THE ALEXANDER MEMOIRS
1940–1945

THE ALEXANDER MEMOIRS
1940–1945

Earl Alexander of Tunis

Foreword by Shane Alexander

Introduction by James Holland

Frontline Books, London

The Alexander Memoirs 1940–1945

This edition published in 2010 by Frontline Books, an imprint of
Pen and Sword Books Ltd., 47 Church Street, Barnsley,
S. Yorkshire, S70 2AS.

Visit us at www.frontline-books.com, email info@frontline-books.com
or write to us at the above address.

ISBN 978-1-84832-567-8

PUBLISHING HISTORY
The Memoirs of Field-Marshal Earl Alexander of Tunis was published
by Cassell & Company Limited (London) in 1962. This edition includes a new
introduction by James Holland and a new foreword by Shane Alexander,
the son of the author. The plate section has been updated with previously
unpublished photographs, which were kindly supplied by the family.

CIP data records for this title are available from the British Library.

Typeset by M.A.T.S. Typesetters, Leigh-on-Sea, Essex
Printed in Great Britain by CPI Antony Rowe

CONTENTS

The Desert

CONTENTS

Two Defeats

Italy

CONTENTS

BATTLE MAPS

ILLUSTRATIONS

between pages 106 and 107

NOTE FROM LORD ALEXANDER
Alex was supremely indifferent to having his photograph taken. Consequently there is a dearth of images of him commanding his troops in the North African and Italian campaigns. Instead some previously unpublished photographs of him taken not long after the war have been chosen by the publishers and are included in this book.

NOTE FROM THE PUBLISHER
The plate section of this edition of this edition of *The Alexander Memoirs* contains many photographs that were used in the original edition, which was published in 1962.

ILLUSTRATIONS

Plate 7   A Valentine Mk2 light infantry tank entering Tripoli in
January 1943; Alex and Montgomery in Italy, November 1943

Plate 8   Alex with General Omar Bradley; General 'Vinegar Joe'
Stilwell

Plate 9   Coming ashore at Salerno with Mark Clark and Dick
McCreery; Alex at a joint services parade in Tunis with Mark Clark
and General Juin

Plate 10   With General John Harding, his loyal chief of staff;
Generals Montgomery, Richardson, Alex, Bedell Smith and Patton
in Sicily.

Plate 11   Alex driving Harold Macmillan around the ruins of the
town of Cassino;
with King George VI on one of his visits to the battlegrounds in the
Liri Valley

Plate 12   With General Anders; Alex with Marshal Josef Tito on
the terrace of the White Palace, Belgrade, 24 February 1945

Plate 13   A gaslit 'summit' conference at the Foreign Office,
Athens, 27 December 1944; final surrender in Italy, 12 noon, 2
May 1945

Plate 14   With Marshal Tolbukhin and Colonel-General Jeltof;
Alex's mobile HQ at Lake Bolsena

Plate 15   Alex addressing his troops; at Buckingham Palace with
the King celebrating the Irish Guards' Golden Jubilee in June 1950

Plate 16   With the Queen and the Earl of Home at the Bowes
Lyon family home, 1950s; inspecting German troops in
Düsseldorf, 1964

PREFACE

Two years ago I returned to the battlefields of North Africa and Italy. I am glad to have undertaken this pilgrimage because I feel that a commander should file for the record the work of his armies in the field. In particular, I was concerned that the Allied campaign in Italy should receive due recognition in history for its contribution to the general victory in the west. Strategic considerations apart, the seemingly unending succession of mountain ranges, ravines, and rivers of the Italian terrain demanded the soldierly qualities of fighting valour and endurance in a measure unsurpassed in any other theatre of war.

Thus it came about that in the autumn of 1960 I left England for Cairo, by way of Athens, and thereafter followed the tank tracks of the British Eighth Army and of the Allied Armies, on the ground or from the air, across the Western Desert into Tunisia, and thence, by way of Malta and Sicily, the length of Italy to Trieste. I was accompanied by my two former Chiefs-of-Staff, Field-Marshal Lord Harding and General Sir Richard McCreery, afterwards to succeed to command of the famed Eighth Army, and by another friend, my collaborator, Major John North, who undertook the task of committing my thoughts to paper.

In the narrative that follows the reader will learn what reflections passed through my mind as I revisited those battle-grounds of the Mediterranean war which, although they have now passed into history, still vividly remain on the horizon of memory for the officers and men who fought over them.

Alexander of Tunis.
Field Marshal

WINKFIELD LODGE
WINDSOR FOREST, BERKSHIRE

FOREWORD

WHEN the author James Robinson wrote a book on my father shortly after the war, he sent a draft to him for comment. My father hardly glanced through the manuscript before replying, 'write whatever you want—it's your book.'

Alex never showed the slightest concern for his reputation preferring, in his memoirs, to concentrate on the military campaigns themselves rather than on the personalities of those involved in them. To this end he revisited the battlefields in North Africa before writing this book.

No one had a clearer vision of those campaigns in North Africa and Italy since it was he who had worked the long hours alone before presenting the plans to his commanders for the necessary briefings. The reader will see in the book's later chapters that he gives full credit to General Anderson of First Army and General Montgomery of Eighth Army, both of whom so ably put his strategies into practice.

I well remember one or two occasions when my school friends, while visiting us at home, grasped any opportunity to ask my father about his experiences in the war, only to be met by a brief, light-hearted comment. He seldom dwelt on the subject (other than asking the boys if they were planning to do their National Service and in which regiments). His interest in the past wasn't great, and the many, many war books he had been given over the years lay unread in the library.

One of my father's chief and indeed abiding interests, which he had had since early youth, was painting in oils. He especially enjoyed his painting excursions to Portugal and other countries in the company of a long-standing family friend, the landscape painter Edward Seago. (He had made the artist his 'Camouflage Officer' during the Italian Campaign and in that capacity Seago produced a number of highly evocative watercolours and pen-and-wash pictures of the treacherous winter conditions there.) My father's other painting companion was Winston Churchill, who once joined him on an extended painting holiday in Italy immediately after the general election in 1945.

National Service was obligatory in the 1950s, but my father was well aware of the changing nature of the armed forces—that is, its growing peacekeeping role—and was completely neutral on my brother or me choosing it as a career. In any case, both of us served for a short period in his regiment, the Irish Guards. He and his three brothers had actively served through—and survived—two world wars, but to the best of my memory none of them ever glorified in it. And neither does this book, which loses nothing in the telling.

SHANE ALEXANDER, 2010

INTRODUCTION

WHEN Field Marshal the Earl Alexander died on Monday, 16 June 1969, so passed one of the last great British heroes. He had been the most experienced battlefield commander of any side during the Second World War, having commanded in combat at every rank of command from subaltern to field marshal. He had fought along the Western Front, commanded German troops in the Baltic in 1919, and had carried out colonial policing duties in the Middle East, India and the North-West Frontier. At the beginning of the Second World War he had been the last officer to leave Dunkirk, had brought the British and India army back from Burma into India, commanded British forces in the Middle East and North Africa, and had been the British and American commander-in-chief when 250,000 Axis troops had been captured with the German and Italian surrender at Tunis in May 1943. He was C.-in-C. in Sicily, and throughout the Italian campaign. It was in Italy that the first German unconditional surrender was signed in May 1945. Post war, he served in Winston Churchill's second government and as Governor-General of Canada, where he granted thousands of displaced European Jews the chance to create new lives.

And then he retired, living out his final years simply. A highly talented artist, he painted and travelled, embarked on building projects and spent time with his family. He rarely looked back. Despite a life that stretched from the reign of Queen Victoria to Elizabeth II, and despite a career that had taken him to the far corners of the globe, which had seen him face death innumerable times, Alex was always a man who looked forward, who embraced the ever-changing world.

No one who met Alex—as he was always known—ever had cause to doubt his integrity; moreover, there were few people more prone to self-deprecation and less likely to blow their own trumpet. Such unassuming modesty had been drummed into him as a child, a childhood in which he had been brought up to respect notions of honour, duty and impeccable manners in all things and at all times.

Born the third son of the Earl of Caledon, Alex's background was distinctly aristocratic. His childhood was spent shooting, fishing and painting on the large Caledon estate in County Tyrone in Northern Ireland. At fifteen he was sent to Harrow, where he excelled at sports. In his final year, he played in Fowler's Match at Lord's, the most famous Eton-Harrow cricket match ever to have been played. From there, he went straight to Sandhurst, passing out in July 1911, aged nineteen. As a fiercely proud Ulsterman, he was determined to join the Irish Guards. The 'Micks' were a young regiment, created by Queen Victoria in only 1900; nearly all its number were Irish. 'They were my bosom friends,' he later said. 'In the Micks there is a great feeling of matiness between officers and men. The Irish love their leaders, as I had found as a boy, and they have natural good manners.' He was yet to excel as a soldier, but was certainly developing into a handsome, highly athletic young man, and the perfect gentleman. Between duties, he found plenty of time to go to dances and the theatre, to hunt, shoot, box and play polo, as well as cricket and golf. He even went motor racing at Brooklands, and in Easter 1914, entered—and won quite effortlessly—Ireland's most famous sprint, the Irish Mile.

The four long years of the First World War developed him as a soldier. He quite openly enjoyed it, despite—or rather, because of—spending almost the entire war with fighting troops. At the First Battle of Ypres in November 1914, he was seriously wounded in the thigh and hand and invalided home. He recovered well and, determined to get back to the front as soon as possible, walked sixty-four miles in one day to prove to a cautious doctor that he was fit enough. Sure enough, by February 1915 he was back and later that summer led his company at the Battle of Loos. His reputation was growing rapidly, notably for his exceptional personal courage, but also for his extraordinary imperturbability and the gift of quick decision. Always leading from the front and with no regard to his own personal safety, he soon had the complete devotion and respect of all those who served under him.

He was wounded twice more, survived the Somme, Cambrai and Passchendaele, and in 1917, aged just twenty-five, became acting Lieutenant-Colonel commanding the 2nd Battalion. By the armistice, he had earned a DSO and bar, an MC, the French Legion of Honour, and had been mentioned in despatches five times. Nor did his combat record stop with the end of war. In 1919, he was sent to command the Baltic Landwehr, part of the Latvian Army, in the war against North Russia. Since most of the men under his command were of German origin, he was unique amongst British commanders of the Second World War in having commanded German troops in battle. Staff college and staff appointments were followed by stints of further action along the North-West Frontier, where his superior at the time, Brigadier Claude Auchinleck, took note of his cool efficiency and began a lasting friendship.

By the outbreak of war in 1939, this gilded officer was one of the army's youngest Major-Generals and commanding 1st Division. He went with them to France, and after the British retreat in May 1940, was left behind to supervise the final withdrawal of British troops, only leaving on 3 June, the last day of the British evacuation.

Remaining in England for the next two years of war, Alex realised that the vast majority of infantry troops under his command were simply not ready for battle. They had no experience of operating under fire, while the junior officers and non-commissioned officers often had only theoretical understanding of lower level tactics. He subsequently began to develop Battle Drills in which junior commanders were taught such tactics in a more practical way, using live ammunition. These tactical exercises would be accompanied by simple instructions that they could drum into the men so that they would react automatically in times of stress—such as, 'down, crawl, observe, fire'. The exercises also provided some kind of battle inoculation, which he recognised was needed before submitting green troops to the terrors of German dive-bombing, shelling and machine-gunning. Thirdly, he realised that it was essential that all troops were battle fit. However obvious this may seem now, the Battle School system had a considerable effect on British troops entering battle from 1941 onwards. Even today, simple, uniform orders, rigorous obstacle courses and exercises using live ammunition are part of the British soldier's training.

It was particularly during his time commanding Southern Command that Alex came to Churchill's notice. The Prime Minister was certainly influenced by Alex's aristocratic back-ground, but also by his calm control and a military record that was second to none. Even in Burma, yet another retreat from defeat, Alex had impressed with his unflappability and ability to make the best of a bad situation.

And he looked the part, too. Modest though he was, Alex had a streak of the dandy about him; he always dressed immaculately.

On leave during the First World War, he spotted a Russian officer wearing a high-peaked cap, with its visor dropping over his eyes. Alex liked the design so much he went straight to his hatter in St James and had him make an exact copy. It was a style he kept throughout his career simply because it *had* style.

There was also plenty of charm. He never swore: describing something as 'tiresome' was the closest he got to cursing, and only once was he ever seen to lose his temper, and that was when some of his men refused to give two dying Germans a drink of water during the Battle of Passchendaele. He drank, but was never drunk; he would sketch and paint whenever he had the chance; spoke a number of languages including German, French and Russian, and was one of a very few British (rather than Indian) Army officers who bothered to learn Urdu whilst in Burma.

He also had a very sound sense of judgement, and perhaps even more importantly, understood the men under his command. He understood how much men could endure and what could be expected of them. He understood that armies need confidence and experience in combat, and that the approach to battle—the preparation and the closing-down of potential stumbling blocks—was the key to victory.

This held him in good stead as Eighth Army began to claw their way back across North Africa in the summer and autumn of 1942. Although Alamein is seen as Montgomery's victory, Alex was Monty's boss and he deserves every bit as much credit for that crucial turning point in British fortunes. Meanwhile, a joint Anglo-American force had landed in north-west Africa, but by early 1943, had become bogged down, with the Americans suffering their first battlefield defeat. Alex was brought in as army group commander and in ten days had reversed the defeat. Eight weeks later came the triumphant final victory in North Africa, and with it a peerage. He had shown a rare ability to handle coalition forces, a skill he continued to demonstrate as he led Allied forces first to victory in Sicily and then into southern Italy.

The battles of Cassino and the landings at Anzio are often seen as low points in the Allied war with Germany, yet the shortage of troops, equipment and above all, shipping, combined with atrocious weather, were factors that were out of Alex's control. What is undeniable is that on 5 June 1944, when Rome finally fell, the month-long campaign had been the Allies' biggest battle to date and had wrought a devastating defeat on the German forces in Italy. Alex's strategy for the rest of the campaign in Italy was one that was subsequently hampered by the precedence given to D-Day and the campaign in North-west Europe. However, during his time as army group commander then Supreme Allied Commander, he managed to not only win a complete victory in Italy but at the same time averted civil war in Greece. In Italy, he commanded twenty-three different nationalities, and not one of his subordinate commanders ever had a bad word to say against him. The Americans, in particular, were frequently at loggerheads with their British allies, but not one US commander had anything other than praise for Alex. Indeed, Eisenhower wanted Alex, not Montgomery, to lead Allied ground forces on D-Day. In war, empathy for others, and the ability to gain the affection and respect of those serving under you, are key attributes at any level of command, but especially important the higher up the chain of command. It is also even more crucial in coalition warfare, as it was from the moment he took command of Eighteenth Army Group in Tunisia through to the end of the war.

Another rare skill of Alex's was his innate understanding of the requirements of every level of command. As Commander-in-Chief Middle East, his job was that of overseer, of co-ordinator. He offered advice to Montgomery, and made suggestions, but did not tell his subordinate how to command the Eighth Army. However, given a more active command in Tunisia, he did exactly that—he *commanded* two armies, directing the course of the battles, and very successfully too. Some of his generals were given a loose rein, others he kept on a tighter leash. He has been criticised in the past for his handling of General Patton during the American's command of US II Corps in Southern Tunisia. Alex changed his orders to Patton six times, yet this was not indecisiveness. It was recognising that Patton, though inspirational, was also impulsive. Alex was not prepared to sit back and let Patton handle II Corps as he saw fit. The change of orders reflected the changing situation and operational requirements, and rather than America-phobic interference, was sound good sense. Interestingly, a few months later, when Patton was an army commander in Sicily and had gained much crucial command experience, Alex was prepared to give him more operational autonomy.

Bragging was anathema to him and, unlike Patton, Montgomery and others, he deplored any kind of publicity about himself, preferring to deflect any praise onto others. It is one of the main reasons that this remarkable man has been, to a large extent, eclipsed by others from that time of global war. It is also why his memoirs are so sketchy; there is more about other people in the book than there is about himself. He was also a man who looked forward, not back; although proud of his achievements and of his numerous honours, he never spent much time thinking or talking about past glories, and very much embraced the ever-changing and rapidly advancing world. By the time he died, he must have been one of the first people in Britain to have had a dishwasher installed in his house, and was also a firm proponent of another new invention: Marks and Spencer's drip-dry shirts. He could be very amusing too, with a keen sense of humour. He kept a book in which he jotted down good jokes or funny incidents, while his war-time letters to his children are filled with wry humour and skilfully drawn cartoons. And these were often penned at times when the pressures of command were at their most intense.

In his time, Field Marshal Alexander he was one of the greatest generals of his age, and it is important that he is not forgotten. He made his mistakes, but his achievements were considerable. More than that, however, his modesty, self-deprecation, and his profound sense of honour and duty, are worthy of our respect and admiration. Certainly, there has been no-one like him since.

JAMES HOLLAND, 2010

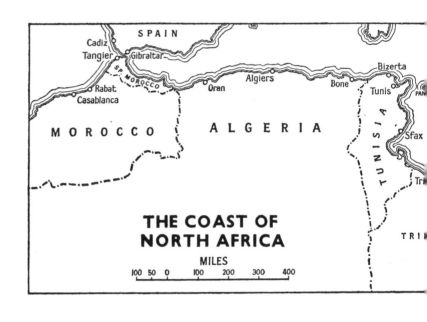

THE COAST OF
NORTH AFRICA

MILES

100 50 0   100   200   300   400

The Desert

I

RETURN TO THE WESTERN DESERT

IN THE autumn of 1960 I returned to the desert. Eighteen years vanished as early morning mist is banished by the sun. I saw again the beautiful blue of the sea—a blue so vivid that if it were put down on canvas it would look unreal—and those marvellous white sand dunes, and felt the wind that quietly blows from the sea: all these brought back the past to me vividly.

One had forgotten the great distances until one saw them again. The desert looked so utterly empty now, as if nothing could ever have happened there. Eighteen years ago the ground where we stood was teeming with activity; now it was all so silent; nothing apparently lives or grows in the desert except the scrub—though I did see a solitary bird. Nothing but the sand, the empty space, and the wind, and here and there a nomad Arab's tent and an occasional camel. One would think it had all been left undisturbed for thousands of years, until one comes across a souvenir or two: the rusted remains of a bully beef tin, an old piece of telephone wire—the little odds and ends that mark the old battlefield.

I looked around the site of our Mena camp on the edge of the desert outside Cairo, with its truly magnificent view over the Western Desert towards the battle-front. Here it was that I established the operational section of my headquarters when I took over the Middle East command; here, too, General Auchinleck, with a few of his senior staff officers, had started his own camp before he went forward to take over personal command of the Eighth Army towards the end of June 1942; but before I reached Cairo in August 1942, the camp had been dismantled.

The site had looked pretty derelict when I arrived; and now, in the October of 1960, could only be identified by our old stone H.Q. mess. Its doors are locked and its windows shuttered; but it

3

has obviously been repaired over the past years, and, no doubt, somebody has made it a home, because there is a caretaker living in what used to be our old kitchen. He is a simple Arab, with a small son, and hens and chickens and a dog: and a highly decrepit Jeep—last remaining vestige of the panoply of war!

Where the tents stood, just below the mess hut, there is nothing but sand, except for a few silted hollows where tents had been dug into the desert. But there were those little depressions that give away one or two sites where perhaps some pit had been dug deeper than the rest. The great Pyramids which stand looking down on the old site must have seen many such military encampments in the generations gone by. Perhaps Napoleon, when he visited the Pyramids, spent a night in their shadow, as did we of the Eighth Army who rested there eighteen years ago.

I saw again that famous feature called Ruweisat Ridge, which was the very backbone of our defensive position, along with another ridge four or five miles to its south and running almost parallel with it—the Alam Halfa ridge: the key—indeed, as seen from the ground, the obvious key!—to the whole of our defensive system. But what is interesting is that, looking over the ground as seen from El Alamein station and thereabouts, one finds that it all looks appallingly flat, with those ridges hardly apparent to the eye. Yet once you get up on them you find that those few feet, sometimes no more than fifty, at the most two hundred, give a tremendous view over the whole countryside.

Time and sand antiquate all things: there are one or two old sites where guns were dug in, but the fox-holes and the slit-trenches have all disappeared. Over the years the sands, blown by the never-failing wind from the sea, have rubbed them out.

It is dangerous, I am told, to wander off the well-established tracks, which only the local guides can tell you about. The fact is that the ground is still sown with mines; and there are still many signs of old tracks used by the Eighth Army.

We went on to look at the Italian war cemetery at Alamein. In the small museum alongside it there is a good photograph of Rommel. I thought, however, that his baton was much too big!

By the courtesy of the Egyptian Government I was given permission to fly over the old battlefield; it is a prohibited area, and aircraft are not normally allowed to go nearer to the coast than ten miles. So there we were, flying up the desert road at about a

4

thousand feet on a cloudless day when visibility could not have been better.

I have indicated that, on the ground, there was really little to show that a great battle had been fought in the desert and that two armies had once been locked in deadly combat for months on end. But from the air the veil protecting mother earth becomes transparent, and much is revealed which it takes no trained military eye to pierce. There, clearly, are the outlines of slit-trenches, gun-pits, tracks, and all the other scars of warfare.

What are equally surprising are the little patches of Arab cultivation dotted about the desert near the coast. These were unnoticeable on the ground, and understandably so, because the seed which had been sown was beneath the soil, and was only waiting to be brought to life by the first rains, when the wheat or barley would spring into leaf overnight.

A mile or so south from the desert road lies the little hamlet of Burg El Arab, not far from where Eighth Army Headquarters used to be, by the white sand dunes. Here lived one of those expatriate Englishmen, a local celebrity. He had served the British Crown in Egypt, and when he retired he made his home in the Western Desert among the Arabs, far away from Cairo and Alexandria.

He had built himself a comfortable stone house and cultivated a fine garden; he did much for the local population, and among them he was a beloved figure. In dress and appearance he was the perfect example of the old-fashioned country squire: unmistakably English even though he lived among the Arabs of the desert and gave one the impression of never seeing or speaking to one of his fellow-countrymen from one year's end to another.

I met him during the war. Someone said to me, 'You know, an old Englishman lives up there in Burg El Arab. His name is Jennings Bramly and he's quite a character.' So I went to see him one day and had tea with him. It was very much a nineteenth-century English home, with a tiger-skin on the floor, with pipes and books and comfortable armchairs and an open fireplace. I don't know why he threw away civilization; or perhaps I should say that he brought it with him to his well-ordered house at Burg El Arab, where it was his delight to entertain his English friends.

So it was that Major Wilfred Jennings Bramly lived but a few miles behind the battle-front, and he certainly had no intention of moving, whichever way the fighting went. The tide of war, in fact, lapped his doorstep. I am sure he would never have handed in his gun to the enemy if the Germans had been victorious; but time and age compelled him to hand in his gun to his Maker. He died quite recently after a long and honourable life.

Our air trip over the desert did not alter my conception of the campaign itself in any detail. I had seen the other side of the hill before, of course, when we were advancing: I had my advanced camp with the Eighth Army, and I was always going backwards and forwards to the front. When we reached Sollum I began to use an aeroplane. I know it all so well because I had covered the ground so often by car and air.

I don't think there was a moment when I wished I had done something else during the campaign. All the time we were pushing the enemy back; we were winning. That is the most delightful feeling of all—the feeling of exhilaration that accompanies the victorious advance.

My return to the desert gave me much on which to reflect; and we had chosen a most appropriate day on which to see the battlefield again. It was exactly eighteen years before that the battle had opened, and it was also the day of the Ceremony of Remembrance at the El Alamein cemetery. And a very beautiful cemetery it is, too: so simple, with its more than 7,000 graves of our fallen comrades, and the names of another 12,000 commemorated in the building itself.

There lie the warriors of the great battle that saw the tuning of our fortunes in October 1942.

We visited Tunisia next, flying *en route* over Marble Arch—the one in the desert. One of the few remaining memorials of the Mussolini régime, it was a famous landmark for the air forces and troops of the Eighth Army. It is a triumphal arch bestriding the road, and Mussolini built it before the war to mark the frontier between Tripolitania and Cyrenaica. The spot is the site of an ancient legend.

In the days when Carthage held what is now Tripolitania and the Greeks held Cyrenaica there was a dispute about the boundary. To settle the matter it was agreed that two Greek runners should set off from Apollonia and two Carthaginians from Tripoli, and that the boundary should be fixed where they met.

They met where Marble Arch now stands, but as the Greeks thought that the spot was too far to the east they refused to accept the verdict of the race—unless the Carthaginians undertook to bury their two runners alive at the meeting-place. The two Carthaginians were brothers, and in their patriotism they agreed to this barbaric proposal. Legend has it that they lie side by side, their bones buried in the sands of the desert at Marble Arch on the frontier between Tripolitania and Cyrenaica.

I visited the house which I made my temporary headquarters after we were in possession of Tunis, the charming Moorish house at La Marsa that has been the residence of the British Consul-General for more than a hundred years. But in those war days I still slept in my caravan, which had come all the way from Cairo.

I went to the corner of the olive grove, adjoining the house, and stood beneath those old trees where, seventeen years before, 'my caravan had rested'; and I thought, strangely, not of great events but of the trivial comedy of the night when I returned to my caravan, after dinner, to find my bed swarming with ants that had entered the window on an olive branch. To put a stop to this unwelcome invasion, I soaked a rag in paraffin, tied it round the offending branch, and lit it. Then I went to bed. But soon the smell of burning woke me up—the dried-up trunk of the ancient olive tree was smouldering and about to envelop me and my caravan in flames. Not a peaceful olive branch! However, a generous dose of cold water did the trick.

My last sight of this historic countryside was from the air.

After one passes over the ancient Arab town of Kairouan the hills around Enfidaville are quickly reached. The country becomes green and mountainous, with here and there the rich farms of the French settlers. Suddenly one realizes that the desert is now left behind. One has passed, with mixed feelings, from an old world into a new.

What is the attraction in endless wastes of sand and desolation? It is not simply nostalgia for old battlefields of years gone by; to my mind nostalgia has little to do with it: the desert lands have some peculiar fascination that has attracted mankind throughout the ages. It may be that man feels a sense of freedom in great open spaces. Time there is no longer the taskmaster; we are one with Nature at its simplest. There is a grandeur in wide stretches where the eye can see no limit to its vision.

And what is more moving than a night under a starlit sky, when earth and heaven seem united in one great presence? What is more beautiful than passing shadows over distant horizons, or the sound of wind over rock and sand? These are Nature's gifts, and they belong to the desert. The tumult and wrath of warfare can mar the grandeur of the desert silence only for a time. When the noise of fighting dies down, when man has had his say, the desert sands resume their quiet and silent dignity as if they had never been disturbed.

There is nothing like this elemental force of nature for making us realize that man is puny. Some may fear the realization; others tend to accept it with reluctance. But all of us have a strange and fearful respect for it—and I for one know a curious nostalgia for those desert wastes when I find myself once again amidst the noise and fret of modern life.

A month or so after the Tunisian victory Mr. Churchill and General George Marshall, the United States Army Chief of Staff, with a notable entourage, visited Algiers and Tunis to discuss the further prosecution of the Mediterranean war. During his stay in Tunis the Prime Minister said to me: 'I want to speak to as many soldiers as you can muster for me.' It seemed to me that one could not have a better place than the old Roman theatre, and I therefore told the staff to prepare it—it held 45,000 men or something like that. But the day before the Prime Minister arrived they came to me and said that it would never do because the acoustics were so bad. My reply was that the acoustics couldn't be as bad as all that: the Romans built these theatres, and they knew all about acoustics. In an amphitheatre, of course, with a sunk arena for gladiatorial and other spectacles, acoustics weren't a problem.

They said, 'Well, you come and listen.' So I went down, and what did I find? They had fitted the theatre with microphones and loudspeakers, and, of course, the reverberations were dreadful. I said, 'Take away these things and try it without them.' It worked like a charm. You had only to stand on the stage and whisper and you could hear just as well as the Romans when they held their great assemblies.

The Prime Minister's experience on a subsequent visit to Carthage, in December 1943, was not so happy. For the second time in ten months he was stricken with pneumonia, and his doctor, Lord Moran, had to send to Cairo for a specialist in the disease, Dr. Bedford, who knew all about the then new drug called M & B, from the initials, of course, of the firm that made it.

Thanks to the care of Lord Moran and Dr. Bedford, and by M & B, Winston was sufficiently cured to attend a small dinner-party that included his wife, his daughter Sarah, his son Randolph, Moran, Bedford, and myself. Then at the end of dinner Randolph rose and proposed this extremely neat toast: 'Ladies and gentlemen, let us rise and drink to my father's health and his remarkable recovery, which is entirely due' (turning first to Lord Moran and then to Dr. Bedford) 'to M & B.'

II

THE WAR IN NORTH AFRICA

CAIRO, AUGUST 1942

EARLY in August 1942 I was told to go at once to Cairo to take over command of the Middle East from General Sir Claude Auchinleck. Mr. Churchill, the Prime Minister, and General Sir Alan Brooke, Chief of the Imperial General Staff, were still in Cairo when I arrived, concluding a mission which was to yield notable results.

It is my view that the Prime Minister showed great powers of leadership in thus going out to the Middle East and making the changes which he believed to be essential. I know—because he told me—that he disliked intensely having to relieve Auchinleck. 'You know,' he said, 'it is like killing a magnificent stag.'

On the morning of 8 August I had a private interview with Mr. Churchill and the Chief of the Imperial General Staff; and two days later the Prime Minister handed me my directive, written in his own hand. It ran thus:

> 1. Your prime and main duty will be to take or destroy at the earliest opportunity the German-Italian Army commanded by Field-Marshal Rommel together with all its supplies and establishments in Egypt and Libya.
>
> 2. You will discharge or cause to be discharged such other duties as pertain to your command without prejudice to the task described in paragraph 1, which must be considered paramount in His Majesty's interests.

Strangely, as I studied the directive, I remembered the queer feeling of exhilaration which I had had when I was ordered to the

BRITISH EMBASSY,

CAIRO.

Directive to General Alexander
Commander in Chief in the Middle East

———————

1. Your prime & main duty will be to take
or destroy at the earliest opportunity the German-
Italian Army commanded by Field Marshal
Rommel together with all its supplies &
establishments in Egypt & Libya.

2. You will discharge or cause to be discharged
such other duties as pertain to your Command
without prejudice to the task described in
paragraph 1, which must be considered paramount
in His Majesty's interests.

W.S.C.
10. Aug. 42

A.F.B.
C.I.G.S.
10.8.42

Mr. Churchill's Directive

Middle East, a premonition that at last our fortunes were about to change.

It was, no doubt about it, a completely irrational feeling. To put it mildly, the military situation did not look good. Our forces in the Western Desert had been defeated by Rommel and as far as I knew were clinging on to the last defensive positions which covered the Nile Delta. In addition, I had been through some trying and difficult experiences. For me the war so far had been nothing but defeats, rearguard actions and efforts to stave off disaster. I thought of Dunkirk and of our efforts after Dunkirk, when I commanded the south of England and had to secure, with inadequate forces and equipment, the home shores against invasion. And there had been the campaign in Burma, in which we were hard put to it to save our forces from annihilation.

Always I had thought—like millions of my countrymen—that we would come through victorious in the end, even if I could not quite see how or when. But now, with my assumption of command in the Middle East, my feelings were tinged with a new confidence. Quite simply, it seemed to me that the tide in our fortunes was about to change: at last we were going to turn from defeat to victory.

In Cairo I was put up at the British Embassy. Winston and Brookie were there, too, busy with conferences, and so I had time to look around and take in the atmosphere.

There were many troops in the Cairo area: too many, I should have thought. The great majority of them had been in action in the desert, and they looked tough and fit enough, but it struck me that they lacked something of the cheerfulness and confidence which one usually associates with our soldiers. They were, in fact, not in good spirits. From my talks with various officers and men I formed the impression that something had gone wrong which they couldn't understand—they were bewildered, frustrated, fed up. I know that Winston has observed that, after a visit to the front three days before my own arrival, he found 'the troops were very cheerful'. But who wouldn't cheer up at the sight of Winston and his cigar?

Among the troops he visited were the Australians, who were naturally very pleased to see him. As he drove slowly along they were continually calling out to him: 'Good on you, Winnie—give us a cigar!' And being Winston Churchill he took out his cigar case and offered it. In no time it was empty, and when he returned from the visit he bemoaned his generosity, saying: 'My lovely cigars—they have taken all my lovely cigars!' Not, of course, that he really begrudged one of them.

There was one matter in Cairo that was of some interest to me. Although I flew my C.-in-C's flag on my car as soon as I assumed command, I was quite ignored by the men—I very rarely got a salute or any recognition. I was tempted to issue an order about this lack of discipline and, indeed, military bad manners; but I thought it wise not to pursue the matter in view of the prevailing temper.

Many of the soldiers I talked to had taken part in victorious advances which had led them to Benghazi and beyond, and had then been pushed back: for months, of course, the desert campaign had been a see-saw between the Eighth Army and the Afrika Korps. And the final result of this contest of arms, when I arrived in Cairo, was, as I have said, that we were back on the final ditch of resistance.

During these conversations I detected, not unexpectedly, a belief that Field-Marshal Rommel, who had commanded the German forces in Africa since their first arrival in February 1941, was a wizard of the battlefield: his publicity build-up had been enormous. There is no question that the Field-Marshal was a most able battle commander and a fine tactician for an independent force like the Afrika Korps, but it was hardly necessary to attribute to him preternatural gifts in order to explain his successes. Incidentally, he was a very chivalrous enemy. I am told that when he took wounded prisoners he would go round the hospitals and praise them for having put up a good show, thereby sustaining and extending, no doubt, the Rommel legend.

That legend contributed a lot to the Eighth Army's widespread belief in the invincibility of the Afrika Korps, the debilitating effect of which was possibly reinforced by that curiously seductive and nostalgic song about Lili Marlene, which, it seems, 'lulled both armies to sleep'.

Now, with the Prime Minister emphasizing the 'need of a new start and vehement action to animate the whole of this vast but baffled and somewhat unhinged organization', and in the light of his own vehement intervention, it seemed probable that the Eighth

Army would have fewer opportunities of surrendering to Lili Marlene's charms.

One of the first things that struck me when I arrived in Cairo was that as well as the many troops who should have been in the desert, the whole of Middle East Command was housed in the city. I have never thought that the operational staff of a headquarters should be stationed in a city—certainly not Cairo, with its restaurants and clubs, its places like Shepheard's Hotel, its manifold distractions. It was all too much divorced from the battlefield. And it stands to reason that the fighting men living in the most primitive conditions, aside from the danger of being in the front-line, must feel some resentment at the fact that their superiors are living something of a life of luxury, or with luxuries near at hand.

I remember very clearly from the First World War, when I was a front-line soldier in the Irish Guards, that our superior commanders and their staffs lived in the great châteaux of France and Belgium, with little opportunity of knowing intimately the conditions in which their troops were fighting. The commander should ensure that his troops shall see him and feel that he has their interests at heart; but throughout my service as a regimental soldier from 1914 to 1918, no commander above my brigade commander ever visited my front-line sector. I realize, of course, that other junior commanders may have been more fortunate.

So it happened that when I assumed command of the Middle East I ordered certain key personnel from both the operational section and the administrative side of my headquarters staff into the Western Desert, and tents and huts were erected just west of the Pyramids. Of course, the great administrative services had to be left in Cairo to deal with the posts, railways, hospitals, and control of our base installations.

At Mena camp we were quit of the relaxing atmosphere of Cairo and could get the feel of the desert where our fighting men were. Here, too, was the beginning of the road which led to the front, known as the Desert Road.

The camp was simplicity itself, just a few bell-tents dug into the sand two or three feet deep and cemented, and a few simple pieces of furniture—a camp bed, a washing-stand and perhaps a rug on the floor. The mess hut was a plain stone building erected by the Royal Engineers.

Later, in order to ensure close personal contact with the commander of the Eighth Army and the commander of the R.A.F., whose operational H.Q. lay alongside that of the Army, I followed the example of my predecessor and arranged for the setting-up of a small advanced mobile H.Q. It consisted of a mess and a few tents, with the necessary signals, transport, and so on, and it was installed in proximity to H.Q. Eighth Army. Thus I and my staff could visit this advanced post and keep in close touch with Eighth Army without adding any burden to them. Full use of this camp was made by myself and my staff; and it remained in existence until the end of the war. It was called Caledon Camp—after my home in Ireland.

Anyway, there I was, in the middle of August 1942, in Cairo. The time had come when a completely new command structure had to be set up.

True it is that the old command had done a magnificent job in stemming the Axis advance at Alamein; but an entirely new approach was necessary to overcome the Rommel legend and, with it, the Afrika Korps. And that brings me to the newly appointed commander of the Eighth Army, the general who was soon to win the confidence and affection of that sorely tried army.

'MONTY'

I first met Monty when he came to the Staff College as a teacher of tactics during my second year there as a student—that would be in 1926. Then, in 1935, when he was an instructor at the Staff College in Quetta, he brought along some of his students to learn something of our tactics and operations against the tribesmen on the North-West Frontier, with whom we had been engaged.

I didn't meet him again until the beginning of the Second World War, when he was the keen, capable, energetic commander of 3 Division, which was on my left flank when I was commanding 1 Division. It would not be true to say that he was aggressive, but he did like to assert that this was the way 3 Division did things, and that this was the way to do it—it was the best way, indeed, the only way, and so on and so on.

In 1940, when I took over Southern Command, I found his corps under me, and he himself was splendid: a fine commander, a practical commander, and one very keen on physical fitness.

Yet I can't disguise that he was not an easy man to deal with; for example, administrative orders issued by my staff were sometimes objected to—in other words Monty wanted to have complete independence of command and to do what he liked. Still, no serious difficulties arose over these very minor disturbances; he was always reasonable when tackled.

Eisenhower told me something about Monty that puts the thing in a nutshell. Ike's staff had issued some order that Monty had ignored, or refused to carry out, and Ike said to him, 'But don't you ever obey orders?' Monty replied, 'If I don't like them I'll go as far as I can in disobedience and try to bluff my way through. But, of course, if I can't get what I want, then I must submit in the end.' In other words, he is one of those people who will always try it on.

It is well recognized that Monty had a great respect for Field-Marshal Alanbrooke, who sometimes had to protect him from the Prime Minister's impatience and never tried it on with him. (I remember that during the latter stages of the North African campaign Winston said to me, with a twinkle, 'Monty? Monty's on the make.')

In the desert Monty wore his black beret with the two badges, and King George VI objected to this irregularity in dress. Monty's answer was that he didn't do it for self-advertisement but in order that the troops would recognize him when he went round the front.

Montgomery is a first-class trainer and leader of troops on the battlefield, with a fine tactical sense. He knows how to win the loyalty of his men and has a great flair for raising morale. He rightly boasted that, after the battle of Alamein, he never suffered a defeat; and the truth is that he never intended to run the risk of a defeat; that is one reason why he was cautious and reluctant to take chances. There is, however, much to be said for his attitude when we consider that, up to October 1942, we had not won a single major battle since the start of the war—except Archie Wavell's operations against the Italians and some local victories against the Axis forces in the Western Desert.

Monty has a lot of personal charm—I always like him best when I am with him. Yet he is unwise, I think, to take all the credit for his great success as a commander entirely to himself; his prestige, which is very high, could be higher still if he had given a little credit to those who had made his victories possible, and there are those besides his own fighting men to whom he owes something.

He was probably always rather a lone wolf—opinionated, ambitious, difficult and not a good mixer. If his wife had lived, her influence over him would have made him more human; when he was so tragically bereaved he retired very much into his shell, to devote his life to his profession. I remember his saying to me, 'One only loves once, and now it is finished.'

As far as I know, he has few intimate friends; that is probably why, being still full of restless energy, he travels round the world on missions which are bound to have a political implication—a role for which he is not suited at all.

Personally, I owe Monty a lot—as we all do.

THE NEW EIGHTH ARMY

As my Chief of Staff I chose General McCreery, who at the time was Major-General, Royal Armoured Corps; and I came under fire from General Auchinleck over the appointment. With characteristic loyalty to one of his old friends, the Auk quite brusquely assailed me for not accepting his own nominee.

Dick McCreery had been my chief staff officer when I commanded 1 Division at the beginning of the war. He was one of those rare soldiers who are both exceptionally fine staff officers and fine commanders in the field. He and I saw eye to eye on military matters; he was, too, my trusted friend and companion whose wise advice and companionship meant much to me. Later, in Italy, General McCreery commanded the Eighth Army with conspicuous success. Events were to prove that I had chosen wisely.

McCreery was an armoured warfare expert who had been sent out to the Middle East by the War Office in the spring of 1942, possibly in the expectation that he might be able to bring about an abandonment of the 'Jock column' type of warfare that had bedevilled the Eighth Army's battlefield tactics.

However, he was never consulted by the Middle East Command at the top level; and when I arrived in Cairo he had just been sacked because of his intransigent opposition to the latest of many ideas for the reorganization of the Eighth Army. Each division was to form two or three 'artillery' columns, protected by tanks and mobile infantry, which were to 'dart in after locating the enemy and subject Rommel to heavy concentrations of artillery fire, and then move again before they could themselves be attacked'. McCreery had stuck to his views and refused to endorse this latest proposal for the organization of the armour. It so happened that when I looked in on Middle East H.Q. I found him alone in his room, awaiting a passage to England. I was happy to rescue him from his predicament.

My farewell meeting with the Auk, with whom I had served on the North-West Frontier of India just before the war, where he brilliantly conducted punitive operations against the tribesmen, was most cordial.

I cannot recollect that we discussed matters of great moment—though I do recall his insistence on the Eighth Army's being kept 'intact'. In any event on an occasion like this one is always conscious that one has been sent along as the new broom; and I do not imagine that the newcomer can be reproached for being tactful enough to avoid discussion of his predecessor's ideas—which, he has to assume, have gone into the discard. Quite certainly our conversation, for a reason which would have given rise to embarrassment, did not touch on the future planning of the old Eighth Army staff.

When I met the Ambassador, Sir Miles Lampson, now Lord Killearn, the first thing he said to me was: 'I am here to serve you military chaps and to do everything I can to look after your base and to help you in every possible way with the Egyptians.' It was a gesture I appreciated, and I responded by taking the Ambassador completely into my confidence.

When I took over command it was all too obvious that the Alamein position was indeed the last ditch in the defence of our base in the Delta—without which the Eighth Army would be powerless to operate as an effective force. In my despatch I wrote: 'It was fairly generally well known that, in the last resort, the Army would retreat again, in accordance with the theory that it must be kept in being.' This theory made no sense to me. And for this reason.

At that time the ports of the Middle East were handling more than 400,000 tons of military stores a month; around 300,000 troops and half a million civilians were employed in rear services, and contracted labour represented about a million and a half more. All talk of 'the defence of the Delta'—for which preparations had been laid on by my predecessor—I found quite unrealistic. If Alamein was lost, the Delta was indefensible and all preparations for its individual defence represented misdirected effort, even as a preliminary to withdrawal. Any such withdrawal—as originally contemplated—'eastwards into Palestine with the greater part of the forces and southwards up the Nile valley with the remainder' would have assumed the proportions of an exodus undreamed of even by biblical standards. In short, without a secure base the Eighth Army must inevitably have ceased to be an army. And, further, the political repercussions of such a move on the Egyptians and everyone else in the Middle East would have been profound.

Again I quote from my despatch: 'The soldier who has been forced to retreat through no fault of his own loses confidence in the higher command; because he has withdrawn already from several positions in succession he tends to look upon retreat as an undesirable but natural outcome of a battle.' This reading of the situation in August 1942—and it is not intended as a reflection on the soldiers—remains my judgement today. Anyone can be forgiven for 'looking over his shoulder' if he is aware that preparations have been made for a possible retreat.

My first step in restoring morale, therefore, was to lay down the firm principle, to be made known to all ranks, that no further withdrawal was contemplated and that we would fight the coming battle on the ground on which we stood. General Montgomery fully concurred in this policy, and communicated it to the Eighth Army H.Q. staff at a meeting held on the second evening of his arrival; and it went out to him as a written directive when I formally took over the Middle East command.

There is no doubt at all that Montgomery, during his address, gave brilliant emphasis to the agreed policy. He informed his audience that he had ordered all withdrawal plans to be burnt, that the defence of the Delta meant nothing to him, that all resources earmarked to that end were to be used to strengthen the Eighth Army. When, as his next move, he ordered back the transport that had been laid on for a possible withdrawal—and the story at the time was that every man had reserved himself a seat!—the soldiers were left in no shadow of a doubt that the new command meant business.

The next stage was to reorganize the Eighth Army, and this task Montgomery undertook with characteristic drive and self-confidence. Henceforth battle groups ceased to exist 'even as an expression'; divisions which had been broken up into 'Jock columns' were re-formed to fight as divisions; tip-and-run tactics were over. An intensive training programme was started and a reserve corps—to consist primarily of armoured divisions—formed. With fresh formations and the Sherman tank, new to the battlefield, plus much artillery and ammunition, we were reaching the stage when we could take on the Germans and Italians on equal terms, if not, in fact, with superior material forces.

Montgomery was busy planning for the battle of Alamein. It was to be preceded by the defensive battle of Alam Halfa.

III

TWO BATTLES

ROMMEL AT ALAM HALFA

T HE plan (as I wrote in my despatch) was to hold as strongly
as possible the area between the sea and Ruweisat Ridge and
to threaten any enemy advance south of the ridge from a
strongly defended and prepared position on the Alam Halfa ridge.
Here I must at once note that the follow-up sentence in my
despatch reads: 'General Montgomery, now in command of Eighth
Army, accepted this plan in principle, to which I agreed.' This
particular sentence—which, incidentally, hardly hangs together—
has been much quoted against Montgomery; but it does not appear
in the original typescript of the despatch, which I hold, and how it
got there is, at this time of day, a matter for unprofitable surmise.

Some twenty miles to the south of Alam Halfa—the total length
of the front is about forty miles—is an impassable salt marsh
known as the Qattara Depression. It was obvious to any well-
trained military mind that with the area between Ruweisat and the
sea strongly held, an enemy advance could only be attempted
between Alam Halfa and the Depression; and any such advance
could not be sustained without extreme peril while the defending
forces on and below the ridge remained intact.

From reports submitted by my Intelligence and from personal
observation I am satisfied that a 'large and elaborate stronghold,
similar to those in the Alamein position itself; defended by wire
and minefields', had been built on the Alam Halfa ridge in July
1942. Thus I have no doubt at all that the defensive potentiality of
the ridge was obvious to my predecessor in the Middle East Command. It was certainly obvious to me, and I have no doubt that it
was equally obvious to the new commander of the Eighth Army,
General Montgomery.

Recently there has been discussion whether or not General Montgomery 'adopted' as his own the plan evolved by his predecessor for the action that was shortly to be fought—actually within little more than a fortnight of his taking over command— in defence of the Alamein position.

I cannot conceive that Montgomery is likely to have been in the least interested in other people's ideas on how to run the desert war; and in my own conversations with General Auchinleck, before taking over command, there was certainly no hint of a defensive plan that at all resembled the pattern of the battle of Alam Halfa as it was actually fought.

I would here interpolate a note addressed to military historians who are rightly meticulous in their examination of phraseology— particularly in despatches—and who have directed their attention to the paragraph in my own despatch, from which I have just quoted, relating to 'the plan': a plan, I repeat, based on a key ridge, and, therefore, one that demanded little or nothing in the way of military appreciation—although, as I have already indicated, the actual pattern of the battle was exclusively Montgomery's. Thus I would say that the plan devised itself by its obviousness. When I referred in this particular paragraph to the plan, I was certainly not harking back to any plan formulated by my predecessor.

The plan that Montgomery is alleged to have adopted is outlined in an appendix to the official despatch on the operations in the Middle East from 1 November 1941 to 15 August 1942. This appendix, called 'Appreciation of the Situation in the Western Desert', is dated 27 July 1942. Even excluding a further Appendix A that is not reproduced, it is a document of nearly 4,000 words, on which lengthy score alone, I imagine, it must have received short shrift had it ever come to the attention of the new commander of the Eighth Army.

But, more seriously, there is no mention of this appreciation in the text of the despatch, nor any mention of the key ridge of Alam Halfa in the 'plan recommended'. Instead one reads that 'the essence of the defensive plan was fluidity and mobility'—which runs directly counter to the basic conception of the battle as fought by Montgomery.

In the body of the despatch it is stated that the new defences that had been developed during July were based on a plan of 'giving depth to the El Alamein position' by preparing positions on 'the keys to the defensive zone . . . the three main ridges running east and west'. The despatch continues:

On these ridges, within field artillery range of each other, were built a series of strongpoints designed to deny the essential observation points to the enemy and to preserve them for ourselves. These strongpoints were designed to take garrisons of two battalions and a regiment of twenty-five-pounder guns. But the majority of the field artillery, with its necessary escort of motorized infantry, and all the armoured forces were to be kept mobile to attack the enemy with fire wherever he might appear, using the strongpoints as pivots of manoeuvre and for observation.

The essence of the plan was fluidity and mobility and the maximum use of artillery fire. The defensive zone extended for thirty miles behind our forward positions. If the enemy attempted to pass round it towards Burg el Arab, he was to be delayed by our light armoured forces and mobile artillery groups.

This 'chequer pattern' of defence would appear to bear no resemblance to the battle as fought by Montgomery; nor is any emphasis laid on the ridge of Alam Halfa—the key to Montgomery's battle; and it will be noted that 'all the armoured forces were to be kept mobile to attack the enemy with fire wherever he might appear', whereas Montgomery maintained to the end his policy of avoiding any possibility of his armoured forces being lured into one of Rommel's traps.

The essence of Montgomery's plan was the digging in, hull down, of the 22 Armoured Brigade at the foot of the Alam Halfa ridge-while keeping his extreme south flank mobile. Until he took over command of the Eighth Army in mid-August, this armoured brigade was continually exercised in a 'swanning' role, of the kind that had repeatedly invited disaster in the past. Ninety-two of the 164 new Grant tanks in the forward area—known for their 75-mm. guns as the E.L.H., Egypt's Last Hope—had been concentrated in this one brigade; but they were still less formidable than the new Panzer IVs, with the long 75-mm. gun. Their presence made it the more imperative that British armour should not be drawn into open fighting; and indeed, to quote its commander, the 22 Armoured Brigade maintained its 'firm defensive positions' throughout the battle. Requests to follow up the Germans when their columns started moving westward were refused.

On the day that I took over command—on 15 August—at Montgomery's request, I sent forward the 44 Division to garrison the ridge as a lay-back position. It received orders to develop the positions on the ridge in the greatest possible strength, whereas the 'large and elaborate stronghold' which I have already mentioned was for a brigade only. The fact is that Alam Halfa had now become something more than a theoretical key to the whole Alamein defensive system.

So I would say that the whole controversy about the 'adopted' plan has been nothing more than a beating of the air with words.

When, on the last day of August, Rommel began his advance, Montgomery refused to be lured into abandoning his static defensive on Alam Halfa; General Horrocks, commanding XIII Corps, which took the strain of the battle, was not unmindful of Monty's last-minute warning—'Remember, Jorrocks, you are not to get mauled'; and Rommel duly retreated, after a severe slogging match fought out south of the ridge. The battle lasted through four days and gained for him only four or five miles of desert. But the decision was hardly in doubt after the first day. Here, I feel, General Horrocks has the last word. 'At 1730 hours 15 and 21 Panzer divisions launched an all-out attack on the 22 Armoured Brigade. . . . This was the key to the whole battle. Could the Germans with their superior numbers break through? . . . As the light began to fail the German Panzer divisions withdrew for the night . . . the crisis was over.'

In relation to the forces engaged, the losses on either side were not dissimilar. But in no sense had the Afrika Korps been so seriously mauled as to be incapable of effective retaliation. Nevertheless, any military student—or, for that matter, layman—who examines the diagram of the battle as fought by Montgomery is likely to ask why he refused to order an armoured southward advance from Alam Halfa with the aim of nipping the German thrust and cutting Rommel's communications.

One answer is that easy-looking arrows on 1962 diagrams can afford no conception of the sinister and engulfing and eruptive emptiness of the Western Desert under the fog of war. The other is that it was vital to the future of Allied Mediterranean strategy generally that no chance be taken that might imperil the really decisive battle that still lay ahead.

In my view Montgomery handled this, his first battle in the

Western Desert, with skill and care. Our forces were building up for the grand offensive, reorganizing and training under a new commander and generally re-equipping with better material. Rommel's offensive, designed as a final break-through, resulted in a serious setback to our preparations, held though it was; yet I believe that we were right to hold our hand at Alam Halfa until we were ready to deliver the knock-out blow—at Alamein.

Alam Halfa was a commanding position designed by nature to hold up an enemy attack striking north in rear of our position. To discourage Rommel from a wide encircling movement to the south, a false map of the desert terrain was produced showing very bad going—'heavy sand impassable for tanks'. This map was driven out in an armoured vehicle, which was abandoned between the lines after being shot at—the crew escaped.

According to General von Thoma, commander of the Afrika Korps, who was captured later, Rommel had intended to make a wider encircling movement, but changed his plans to a shorter hook after what he thought was the opportune capture of the faked map.

Of course, like all good stories that verge on the legendary, this particular story has come under the fire of the researchers. Certain German commanders in the operation have been interviewed—usually some years after the event—and, perhaps not surprisingly, have denied that they were misled. I myself would be reluctant to relinquish it. Although von Thoma was actually on the Russian front during this episode, I would say, from my knowledge of the man, that he got the real story when he returned to his head-quarters, which he duly imparted, at the time. Nor is it anywhere on record that he withdrew his opinion.

Alam Halfa had lost us a week; our material losses, though comparatively slight, and the necessary redisposition of troops, had set us back perhaps another week; and I was determined that Eighth Army should have all the time required for training and for the assimilation of its reinforcements. On these grounds I decided to wait until as late as possible for the opening of the Alamein offensive. The actual date was determined by the phases of the moon. The plan must involve a series of infantry attacks against strong defences to gain possession of the enemy's minefields and make gaps in them to pass through the armour. A night assault was obviously demanded; and if the infantry were to be able to lift the mines quickly and accurately, they would need good moonlight. Full moon was on 24 October; and, in agreement with Montgomery, I decided on 23 October as D Day.

I carried out a thorough reconnaissance of the whole front in my car and discussed the plan of attack in all possible aspects with Montgomery. The choice was between an attack in the south, where the enemy defences were rather weaker, which would develop into one more variation on the classic theme of an envelopment of the inland flank; or a straight blow at the north, where the defences were stronger but the results of success would be more far-reaching. The plan that Montgomery finally submitted to me was to make the main thrust in the north, with a secondary attack in the south as a feint to pin down the enemy on this part of the front. A penetration along the coast road would force the enemy away from his communications, putting all the forces south of the breach in imminent danger of isolation.

The hostile front might be compared to a door, hinged at its northern end. To push at the free end might cause it to swing back some way before any serious damage was done; but a successful blow at the hinge would dislocate the whole front and throw the doorway wide open.

ALAMEIN IN RETROSPECT

At Alamein Rommel was utterly defeated but not annihilated: Alamein was a decisive victory but not a complete one.

It is easy to look back after eighteen years and suggest that the Afrika Korps could have been destroyed by a more vigorous exploitation after the break-through, but let us remember the realities of the time.

Monty had his first big command. He was new to the desert. He was fighting a great battlefield tactician in Rommel, whose troops were seasoned warriors: he and they had won some remarkable victories; whereas the Eighth Army had only recently been re-formed and given the material to take on the Axis at better odds; many of our fresh reinforcements were new to desert conditions; and although our Intelligence was good we couldn't know accurately what punch the Germans were still nursing.

At a later stage, when the Eighth Army commander knew what

his troops could or could not do, and so on, Monty might have taken a bigger risk to mop up the Afrika Korps. But in the process he might have had a bad setback—who knows? We must also consider that his motto, not without wisdom, was 'No defeats': in the light of the desert past who dare criticize him for being too cautious? One of his main aims was not to jeopardize the victory he had gained.

There is a further point. British generals are very conscious of the sanctity of men's lives. We are reluctant to sacrifice our troops on a gamble, partly because we have so few to fight with, partly because we lack ruthlessness in this matter. If we are to lose valuable lives we must be sure that the sacrifice is worth while.

The night of 23 October was calm and clear and brilliantly illuminated by an almost full moon. At 2140 hours the whole of Eighth Army artillery, almost a thousand field and medium guns, opened up simultaneously for fifteen minutes against located enemy batteries; it was an extraordinary sight, reminiscent of the First World War, and the intensity of the fire had the effect of silencing almost all the hostile guns. After a five-minute pause fire was resumed at 2200 hours against the enemy forward positions and simultaneously the infantry of XIII and XXX Corps advanced to the attack. The battle was on.

This great battle lasted for eleven days; and on the seventh day, 29 October, I visited the Eighth Army commander at his operational headquarters in the desert, accompanied by Dick McCreery. The moment had now arrived for the final phase, Operation Supercharge, which was to put the armour through the last of the German prepared defences. Not surprisingly, opinion differed as to where exactly this final thrust should be made.

It is an historical illusion that the Eighth Army did not go into the attack at Alamein until it had built up an 'overwhelming' superiority of strength. The battle to date, as we fully anticipated, had been one of gruelling attrition; and on this morning of 29 October Eighth Army had reserve strength enough for only one last big push. Hence the vital nature of the decision that was about to be taken at the meeting attended by, apart from Monty, Dick McCreery and myself, Freddie de Guingand, Montgomery's Chief of Staff, and Oliver Leese, commanding XXX Corps.

The Eighth Army commander appeared to favour an attack as

far north as possible. But Dick McCreery, as an experienced armoured commander, was emphatic that it should go in just north of the existing northern corridor. There is no doubt at all in my mind that this was the key decision of the Alamein battle, nor have I any doubt that Monty was suitably grateful to my Chief of Staff. He himself records: 'The change of thrust line for "Supercharge" proved most fortunate,' though, of course, being Monty, he afterwards informed Eisenhower that never again would he take anybody's advice in the running of a battle! And, so far as I know, he never did—doubtless to the great good fortune of the Army Group he afterwards commanded in north-west Europe.

Some may argue that Monty's master-plan for the battle collapsed because the armour failed to break through the two 'fore-ordained' corridors, which were sealed by powerful anti-tank screens. But nothing in battle can ever be regarded as fore-ordained. I would agree that too great a task was imposed on the armour on the first day of the battle and that there ought to have been two bites of the cherry—a double bombardment. Nevertheless, the essence of the plan was to blow a hole—preferably two holes—in the enemy front. One such hole was blown, at what point makes no matter. The plan worked.

An attrition battle hardly lends itself to master planning. I would say that Alamein was a soldier's battle, and was fought, though with modern weapons, very much in the style of the battles in France in the first war, but with one rather big difference. Alamein casualties averaged out at something over a thousand a day: on the first day of the Somme, in July 1916, they numbered some 60,000.

But Alamein had a political as well as a military object. And those who ask themselves if the battle was necessary should consider certain facts. Three days before Alamein I received the following message from Winston Churchill: ' "Torch" [the proposed landings in North Africa] goes forward steadily and punctually. But all our hopes are centred on the battle you and Montgomery are going to fight. It may well be the key to the future.'

Alamein's immediate political object, in fact, was to influence the French in Algeria and Morocco not to oppose the landings. The strategic plan was to clear the North African shores so that we could open the Mediterranean to our shipping and thereby relieve Malta, which was perilously short of food, and, in a wider strategic sense, to threaten Europe from the south. In the general context of our war strategy in 1942, the battle of Alamein was fought to gain a decisive victory over the Axis forces in the Western Desert, to hearten the Russians, to uplift our allies, to depress our enemies, to raise morale at home and abroad, and to influence those who were still sitting on the fence. The battle at Alamein was very carefully timed to achieve these objects—it was not a question of gaining a victory in isolation.

Before the battle I was worried by the fear that Rommel would withdraw to a firm defensive position at Matruh or Sollum, thereby giving us long communications from Cairo and Alexandria, whilst he would have had his base at Benghazi nearer his back. Any such strategic withdrawal would have strengthened the Axis position in North Africa very considerably, and I would not like to claim that we could then have defeated the Afrika Korps. But fortunately for us Hitler had no use for strategic withdrawals.

I won't say that if the battle of Alamein had not been fought and won the French would have made the 'Torch' landings an even trickier business, but I am quite certain that the British First Army and the United States II Corps could never have taken Tunis and Bizerta unaided.

'Torch' was a long-term, long-distance threat to Rommel's rear; as Rommel himself said, it 'spelt the end of the army in Africa'. However, that end was to prove brilliantly protracted; even when the Germans lost their main base at Tripoli they fought on.

My knowledge of military history and my personal experience convince me that a war is not won by sitting on the defensive. Victory over an enemy can be gained only by vigorous offensive action by all the means at one's disposal; and, in the event, Rommel's retirement had to be imposed upon him by force of arms every inch of the way.

There is one further point. The Casablanca Conference in January 1943 decided that, after Tunisia had been cleared, the operation to open the Mediterranean to our shipping should be completed by the invasion and conquest of Sicily. In making the plans for this operation it was further decided that the campaign in Africa must end by the middle of May in order to give us the chance to bring the Tunisian ports into full use: otherwise it would have to be postponed until August, when the deterioration in weather introduced a serious hazard. This was a difficult timetable to observe. Yet I had Tunis and Bizerta eight days before the allotted date, though with only two days to spare after all resistance in Africa had ceased.

Here was the final dividend of Alamein. Without that victory in November 1942, Allied strategy for 1943 could never have developed the offensive against southern Europe in September of that year.

IV

'TORCH' PAYS OFF

CHURCHILL AS STRATEGIST

B EFORE I record the surrender of Tripoli to the Eighth Army, on 23 January 1943, and the drive on Tunis, I should like to examine one or two aspects of Winston Churchill's strategy. In my view Winston rightly saw the strategic advantages of clearing the North African shores of all enemy forces, to enable us to open the Mediterranean seaways for our shipping to the Middle East and to the Far East.

Furthermore, once in undisputed possession of the North African shore, with all its ports and facilities, we were in a position to threaten the soft under-belly of Hitler's 'European fortress' (a phrase of which the Prime Minister strongly disapproved), thereby forcing on the enemy a dispersion of his forces and gaining the initiative to attack where and when we wished. To achieve success in North Africa Winston took a great risk in sending tanks from the United Kingdom to the Middle East at a time when we were extremely weak at home and in expectation of invasion.

This was a decision in the grand manner. Yet from a purely military point of view the Prime Minister's usual strategy showed certain weaknesses, in that he ignored the principle of concentration of forces at the point and at the time when they could be most decisive. For example, he was curiously enamoured of seizing some quite unimportant objective, such as a few Greek islands in the Ægean, regardless of their future use as a stepping-stone in the conduct of the war and of the fact that such a *coup* would be an administrative burden and tie up valuable fighting units which we could ill spare.

One suspects that in those dark days he wanted any victory over the enemy to announce in the Commons, not only to justify his own leadership but to keep up morale. And why not? I seem to remember that during the Napoleonic wars Pitt went looking round for islands in the Mediterranean which we could take from the French, regardless of their material or strategic value.

Naturally enough, we soldiers regard this kind of activity as not keeping one's eye on the ball. In any military appreciation the first consideration is the objective; when that is decided everything is concentrated on gaining it.

Yet I must admit in our own time, when whole nations are drawn into the struggle for survival, purely military strategy is not enough. Strategy must take account of the feelings and will of the people engaged in war; their morale is an important if not over-riding factor.

Nowadays, therefore, the politicians' idea of strategy and the purely military view of strategy must be closely allied and balanced. This balance, as between chiefs of staff and political chiefs, is not easily achieved. During the last war it worked out pretty satisfactorily in the end, but not without blood, sweat and tears.

Is the answer to the problem to train the politician in military strategy and the military man in political strategy? No. Let each remain an expert in his own field and let the two sides be brought together to hammer out the best solution to a common problem. In any event, the military, in our democratic set-up, are the sub-ordinates of the chosen representatives of the people, and can therefore only advise their political chiefs.

THE DRIVE ON TUNIS

The objectives of the British First Army were the ports of Tunis and Bizerta, some 1,850 miles from Alamein. The landings took place on 8 November; by the end of the month the first dash to capture the ports had expired. Thereafter, for more than four months, the only big movement was the American retreat through the Kasserine Pass in the following February. Throughout these months the Eighth Army was fighting a succession of hard battles through Cyrenaica and Tripolitania. Tripoli itself was captured on 23 January 1943; but the Anglo-American forces were not to enter Tunis and Bizerta until 7 May—and then only with the assistance of two divisions and a Guards brigade from Eighth Army.

I would remark that the 'hard battles' referred to were Monty's battles—not mine. During this period I was able to pay only occasional visits to his front: at that time the Middle East Command extended to Palestine and Trans-Jordan, Syria, Iraq, Sudan, Eritrea. In my view he fought these battles with great skill; and the accompanying maps tell their own story. I would only note that no Eighth Army man I have ever met would acknowledge a pang because of the Army's enforced and final halt, on 29 April, at Enfidaville. In the estimation of these veterans of the desert campaign, the job was done—and it was only a question of helping our First Army, hopelessly bogged down in their wretched mountains!

Nevertheless I feel that I should formally record the extent of Eighth Army's achievements. In six months they had advanced over eighteen hundred miles, and fought numerous battles in which they were unfailingly successful. This would be an astonishing rate of progress even in a civilized country—the equivalent of an advance from London to two hundred miles east of Moscow. In a desert it was even more remarkable. It reflects in particular the greatest credit on the administrative services.

Tripoli was not seriously defended by Rommel; but its capture, three months to the day after the opening of our offensive, marked a definite phase in the African campaign. Tripoli had always shone as a far distant goal in the eyes of the Desert Army since the time when the first armoured cars crossed the frontier wire into Libya on the morning of 11 June 1940. Now the Western Desert belonged to the past—and to history; ahead lay Tunisia—by comparison a European country.

After the Eighth Army had taken Tripoli and was advancing towards the frontiers of Tunisia, Winston Churchill and General Sir Alan Brooke came to the city and reviewed certain of the troops which were not in the van of the advance at that time.

The visitors spent a night or two in my caravan just to the south of the town, off the main road to the airport; and when the Prime Minister was leaving for England he said to me: 'Pray let me have a message which I can read in the Commons when I get back—and make it dramatic and colourful.' So I reported to the effect that Egypt, Cyrenaica, Libya and Tripolitania had all been cleared of enemy forces. The original message is now in the Queen's library at Windsor Castle. It reads:

> General Alexander to Prime Minister. Sir,—The orders you gave me on August 15, 1942,* have been fulfilled. His Majesty's enemies together with their impedimenta have been completely eliminated from Egypt, Cyrenaica, Libya and Tripolitania. I now await your further instructions.

The Allied Expeditionary Force that had come ashore in North Africa on 8 November 1942 was divided into three task forces. They had landed on the west coast of Morocco, north and south of Casablanca, at Oran, and at Algiers. The former two were American; the landing at Algiers, though under American command, included a British brigade group, and it was the intention to build up into Algiers as rapidly as possible the advance elements of the British First Army, under General Anderson. General Eisenhower's mission was first to secure his base in the three assault areas and establish communications between them, and then to launch First Army eastwards from Algiers into Tunisia to seize the ports of Tunis and Bizerta.

The French did oppose our landings; but on 10 November Admiral Darlan agreed to an armistice and ordered all troops in North Africa to cease resistance. At a stroke the unhappy period of hostilities with the French was reduced from a possible three months to two days; and at once General Eisenhower was able to turn his attention to the task of pushing First Army at full speed towards Tunisia. Tremendous difficulties faced it. The distance from Algiers to Tunis is five hundred and sixty miles, by two roads and an indifferent railway; almost the whole of this stretch of country is very mountainous; and First Army, when it began its eastwards advance, consisted only of one infantry division, the 78, reinforced later by an armoured regimental group and two commando and two parachute battalions.

The decision to make a dash for Tunis was undoubtedly correct, though bold; and the advance was pressed by land, sea, and air. Two main attempts were made to capture Tunis. The first succeeded, on 28 November, in reaching a point only twelve miles from Tunis; but our own air forces were unable to give cover, since

* The date should have been the 10th, not the 15th.

34

TO Prime Minister

FROM Gen. Alexander

	Originator's Number	Date	

Sir, the orders you gave on Aug 15d 1942 have been fulfilled. His Majesty's enemies together with their impedimenta have been completely eliminated from EGYPT, CYRENAICA, LIBYA and TRIPOLITANIA. I now await your further instructions.

19 MAY 43

Mr. Churchill said: 'Pray let me have a message which I can read in the Commons when I get back....' (The date should have been 'AUG. 10th'.)

the rain had put all their temporary landing grounds out of action; and we had to withdraw to Medjez el Bab.

This town, as its name 'The Ford of the Pass' implies, is of great strategic importance. It lies on the broad Medjerda river, which breaks out of the mountains at this point to flow into the plain of Tunis through a defile commanded on the west by Gebel Ahmera, better known to our troops—and to history—as 'Longstop'. The bridge that has replaced the ford carries the main road from Tunis to the west. On 22 December, as the first stage of a renewed assault on Tunis, a successful attack was made on Gebel Ahmera. At this moment in time the rain, which had already caused severe difficulties of movement, became torrential for a period of three days. The offensive had to be abandoned. On 25 December the enemy recaptured 'Longstop'. The problem now was to build up forces for a deliberate operation.

Not until the third week in April 1943, by which time the enemy was cut off from his bases in Sicily and Italy, was it possible to deliver the *coup de grâce*. The obvious operation was a direct thrust at the enemy's heart, Tunis, the centre of all his communications and his chief base in North Africa; and the shortest and most direct axis for our attack was from Medjez el Bab to Tunis. But what is obvious to one side is equally obvious to the other, and we had to deceive the enemy about our route. This deception was achieved by a delicate balance of forces. Strength was shown on the chosen axis, but other and considerable strength was developed farther south, where a network of roads leads into the Tunisian plain and where we believed that the enemy would surely be sensitive.

The plan which we developed was to make a strongish attack at this point, and if it was not countered by enemy reinforcement of armour we might well have the opportunity to exploit the move. If, however, he was alarmed by these manoeuvres and drew off his armoured strength from the Medjez el Bal–Tunis front, it would give us the opportunity to make the main and decisive thrust on this our chosen route. In the event the Germans fell for our opening manoeuvre and transferred their main armoured forces to the south.

The diversionary attack started on the morning of 22 April. At once the Germans reacted and put in a violent counter-attack— it struck our strongest point and they suffered heavy losses. The counter-attack provided clear evidence that the Germans were very sensitive in this area; it also showed—more valuably—that they had weakened their forces on the Medjez el Bab front, and, in addition, were not paying attention to the threat of the United States II Corps, which in the north was successfully fighting its way forward towards Bizerta.

For the final phase of the North African campaign I had reinforced the British First Army with the 7 Armoured Division, the Indian 4 Division, and the 201 Guards Brigade, all brought over from the Eighth Army, which was held up by the mountains at Enfidaville and could play no useful part, except to exert pressure and tie down Axis forces. When the final attack went in on 6 May we advanced on a 1,300-yard front, led by the British 4 and Indian 4 Divisions, followed closely by the 6 and 7 Armoured Divisions. The 6 Armoured Division, which had been fighting with the 1 Armoured Division farther south, had moved north under cover of darkness, leaving its area filled overnight with dummy tanks and, of course, leaving behind also the necessary wireless communications to give the enemy the phoney information that there was still a corps H.Q. and two armoured divisions facing him.

In the final break-through on the axis Medjez el Bab–Tunis, the two infantry divisions blew a mile-wide hole in the Axis front, through which passed the two armoured divisions, who covered the distance to Tunis, a matter of thirty-four miles, in thirty-six hours, then swung outwards in wide encircling movements to round up 248,000 prisoners. Only a handful of the enemy escaped the net, and most of these were German marines employed in the ports of Bizerta and Tunis—they escaped to sea in small craft.

I followed the advance fairly closely in my open desert car and saw the German and Italian soldiers being rounded up. Others were driving themselves, in their own transport or in commandeered horse-carts, westwards in search of prisoner-of-war cages. Men who had, so short a time before, been fighting like tigers now seemed transformed into a cheerful and docile crowd, resigned to the acceptance of defeat.

One or two points about this battle may be of general interest. First, after the poor showing of the American troops at Kasserine and, later, at the Fondouk Pass, and, as I saw it, the necessity of finding them a victory to restore their morale and national prestige, I transferred the United States II Corps to the extreme north with

37

the important objective of Bizerta. To help them I gave them the French Moroccan Goumiers, who were experienced mountain troops and great fighters. I hoped that the Americans would take Bizerta at the same time as the British took Tunis, and they did indeed—on the same day!

Secondly, I did not agree with the ideas of General Anderson, the First Army commander, about the conduct of the battle. He wanted the armour, after its original break-through, to mop up the battlefield. I disagreed entirely and gave very strict orders that once the infantry had made the hole the two armoured divisions were to ignore the battlefield just fought over and drive with all speed and energy on Tunis—'the rapier was to be thrust into the heart'. Horrocks, who commanded the corps of attack, was splendid and in entire agreement. We know the result.

My opponent was General von Arnim, and as a prisoner on his way back to General Eisenhower's H.Q. he stayed the night at my field headquarters at Le Kef. I didn't invite him to dine with me— I didn't feel the gesture to be necessary; but I had a special tent and a little mess set up for him so that he could be looked after comfortably and in a manner I considered right and proper of a man in his position. He was, in fact, entertained in the same style as any other guest I might have had, but he was alone with his A.D.C.

When he arrived I had a short interview with him, but I didn't ask him for any information or embarrass him in any way—interrogation could come later.

Von Arnim I found to be a fine, old-fashioned type of German general of distinguished family, an officer who was a gentleman and who had belonged to the 4 Garde Regiment zu Fuss—the same number as my own regiment, the Irish Guards, or 4 Regiment of Foot Guards—in the Kaiser's day. During our short conversation I felt that he was expecting me to say what a splendid fight he and his men had put up, but I'm afraid I disappointed him—we hadn't yet won the war. However, looking back I think it would have been a little more generous of me if I had been more chivalrous.

Finally, there is the not unimportant matter of the reinforcing of the First Army. Monty, in his memoirs, gives the impression that this was his initiative and idea—whether he intended to do so I don't know. But, of course, Montgomery had nothing to do with the attack on Tunis. When, to strengthen the blow, I decided to give First Army the two divisions from Eighth Army, I went over to see Montgomery, and found that, like me, he was not satisfied with the progress on the First Army front. I left it to him to suggest the two divisions and he loyally gave me of his best.

The final victory in Africa was an unusually complete example of the battle of annihilation. Never before had a great army been so totally destroyed. A quarter of a million men laid down their arms in unconditional surrender; 663 escaped. Immense stocks of arms, ammunition, and supplies of all natures were the booty of the victors. Our own casualties in the final battle were fewer than two thousand men. At 1415 hours on 13 May I sent the following signal to the Prime Minister:

Sir, it is my duty to report that the Tunisian campaign is over. All enemy resistance has ceased. We are masters of the North African shores.

V

TWO AMERICAN GENERALS

DWIGHT D. EISENHOWER

THE operations in North Africa in 1942-3 brought me into association with three American soldiers of widely differing characters and temperaments: Eisenhower, Bradley and Patton.

General Eisenhower, who came to us as Supreme Allied Commander, was a professional soldier with all the advantages of a professional military training. He had been General MacArthur's chief of staff in the Pacific, and was obviously highly thought of, but he had never fought on the battlefield in the First World War.

In this context I ask myself if the experience I gained on the battlefield as a junior leader in the First World War helped me as a higher commander in the last war; and the answer is, 'Yes, and yes again.' Tactics alter, but we who fought on the Western Front know what front-line soldiers suffer and feel; we who went through the mill in the First World War know only too well what it means to be shot at and pounded by lethal weapons.

This is not to say that Eisenhower was unappreciative of the front-line soldier's point of view. Nor did he lack understanding of the tactics of modern warfare. But since he was not so conversant with modern methods as were his junior commanders, he very wisely trusted us to fight his battles—and as results proved he was right!

In warfare today a Supreme Allied Commander has much more responsibility on his shoulders than the straight fighting of battles. He finds himself entangled with strategic and political problems, with international relations, and with many other complicated issues far divorced from the front-line. Judging General Eisenhower against this background I think that his was an excellent appointment and that he carried out his assignment with great distinction.

It was not my good fortune to serve alongside Ike when he moved to top command in north-west Europe—and what a transition it was! In February 1945 his armies totalled eighty-five divisions; whereas in February 1942, as commander of the Allied Expeditionary Force in North Africa, his United States II Corps in Tunisia comprised two divisions.

At the Casablanca Conference, which opened on 14 January 1943, it was agreed that the Eighth Army should come under General Eisenhower's command when it entered Tunisia from Tripolitania, and that I, as Ike's deputy, should assume responsibility for the entire conduct of operations in Tunisia by the Eighteenth Army Group, to be composed of the British First and Eighth Armies. The Army Group number, of course, combined the numbers of First and Eighth Armies. The United States II Corps, successively under Generals Patton and Bradley, and the French Corps, under General König, were also to come under my command.

These were, I imagine, halcyon days for Ike, and helped to prepare him for the great strains that lay ahead. At Algiers or Tunis it was a delight to listen to him in quick-fire action at the conference table. Perhaps I should add that, at Casablanca, he informed President Roosevelt and his own chief, General Marshall, that he would be delighted to serve under me in the forthcoming operations. Thus I have every reason, like the American electorate, to like Ike.

Yet I must record—without any bitterness—that he alone was responsible for halting the triumphant advance of my armies in Italy at a key moment in that campaign. In his own book he relates how, from the last week in July through the first ten days of August 1944, he conducted the longest-sustained of all his arguments with 'Prime Minister Churchill'—one session, he notes, lasted several hours. This argument concerned 'Anvil'—later called 'Dragoon'—the codename for the invasion of southern France on 15 August. One of the early reasons for planning this attack was to acquire an additional port of entry through which the reinforcing divisions already prepared in America could 'pour rapidly into the invasion'. The Prime Minister held that the troops could be brought in via the Brittany ports, or might even be better used 'in the prosecution of the Italian campaign with the eventual purpose of invading the Balkans via the head of the Adriatic'. Ike would not accept the Brittany ports and stuck out for Marseilles.

Rightly, as commander of the attack on Germany, he was not prepared to take any chances; and there was no reason at all why he should feel any concern for the future of the Italian campaign. It had started as a secondary front and, despite all Winston's efforts, it appeared to be doomed to remain a secondary front. The only American general who really backed it was General Mark Clark, who has written: 'Save for a high-level blunder that turned us away from the Balkan States and permitted them to fall under Red Army control, the Mediterranean campaign might have been the most decisive of all in post-war history.'

In the operations in Italy I lost seven divisions—four American and three British—to the landings in Normandy. And Operation 'Dragoon' was to entail the switch of another five of my divisions— three American and two French, together with ancillary troops and a considerable proportion of my air strength. The advance of the Fifteenth Army Group to the Po valley was thus inevitably halted: and once across that river the British and American Armies would have constituted a direct strategic threat to southern Germany. In the event, they did not reach the Po until the last fortnight of the war. But reach it they did, despite the fact that in February 1945 I lost to north-west Europe my Canadian I Corps, consisting of two infantry divisions and an armoured brigade, and, a month later, the British 5 Division.

On the political side of the Italian campaign Ike was equally firm. He informed Winston Churchill that it was on military grounds only that he refused to concede the validity of his argument. If the Prime Minister was of the opinion that the Allies should establish themselves in great strength in the Balkans to prevent a Russian occupation and to produce a more stable post-war world, then 'he should go instantly to the President and lay the facts as well as his own conclusions on the table'. Winston did not take up the challenge; and, again, I don't feel that he is to be reproached. It would have been a difficult task: the Americans were just as vague about the Balkans as were many of the British about the islands in the Pacific.

Why then do I charge Ike alone with having delivered a body-blow at the Italian campaign, despite Winston's powerful advocacy? Because, as he records, the United States Chiefs of Staff, following their usual practice, declined to interfere with the conclusions of the commander in the field. Thus the decision lay solely with Ike, who, as I say, felt no concern about the future of the Italian campaign; and much as I admire him I cannot believe that the ultimate formation of the United States Sixth Army Group, following the 'Anvil-Dragoon' operation, represented anything other than an unwise dispersion of force.

The original codename 'Anvil' for the invasion of southern France made some sense; its complement, 'Overlord', was to be the hammer of a vast pincer movement. By 15 August the battle of the break-out in Normandy had been won; a week later every British and American soldier on that front was facing east. Then not even the codename of the operation made sense. Presumably it was dropped for this reason.

Ike had an abiding loyalty to the United States Army Chief of Staff, General George Marshall, who had steadily refused to agree to the 'elimination' of 'Dragoon'; and conceivably Ike's loyalty to his own chief may have influenced his personal decision. For it was General Marshall, when Ike was under fire from Winston over the political significance of Berlin in April 1945, who again intervened and bleakly wrote to the Supreme Commander: 'Such psychological and political advantages as would result from the possible capture of Berlin ahead of the Russians should not over-ride the imperative military consideration which, in our opinion, is the destruction and dismemberment of the German armed forces.' Nor was this key question of Berlin ever formally discussed by the United States and British Chiefs of Staff—the Combined Chiefs.

In fact, the only political direction Ike received came from the new President of the United States, Mr. Harry Truman, who merely instructed him to take a military decision in the field on whether or not to occupy Berlin. Thus here I have every sympathy with Ike—one feels that the political direction of the war failed him at the last critical phase.

Doubtless it is possible to argue—as Ike himself has since argued —that it was pointless to advance on Berlin rather than Berchtes-gaden since, under the terms agreed on the recommendation of the European Advisory Commission, sitting in London between

February and July of 1944, any territory captured by the Allies within the planned Soviet Zone would necessarily be relinquished to the Russians. The fact remains that it was the Russians who staged the Great Surrender, in Berlin, as conquerors of the city— symbol of the defeat of Germany—after Ike himself had negotiated it at his own headquarters in Rheims.

GEORGE S. PATTON, JNR.

I first met General George Patton in Tripoli in 1942. Why he was there I don't know—he probably came to make contact with the Eighth Army and learn something from their operations. No one could fail to recognize him as a colourful character, this fine-looking man who carried a pearl-handled pistol on each hip. He was, like many Americans, friendly and forthcoming, but not in the least aggressive.

My next encounter with him was in Tunisia, where he was in command of the United States II Corps, then operating with the British First Army. At that time I had taken over all the ground forces, my command becoming the Eighteenth Army Group.

Soon after the formation of the Eighteenth Army Group, General Patton, on taking over command of the United States Seventh Army which he was to lead in the invasion of Sicily, handed over command of II Corps to General Bradley; but he remained with it long enough for me to see General Patton and General Bradley together. They were two completely contrasted military characters; the one impatient of inaction, the other unwilling to commit himself to active operations unless he could clearly see their purpose. On one of my visits to the American head-quarters, I was fascinated to hear this characteristic exchange:

> PATTON: Why are we sitting down doing nothing? We must do something!
> BRADLEY: Wait a minute, George! What do you propose we do?
> PATTON: Anything rather than just sit on our backsides!

Both were good soldiers. Patton was a thruster, prepared to take any risks; Bradley, as I have indicated, was more cautious. Patton should have lived during the Napoleonic wars—he would have been a splendid Marshal under Napoleon.

During the invasion of Sicily, when the American Seventh Army landed on the beaches and had quite a sticky time getting ashore, General Patton is reputed to have himself manhandled an anti-tank gun to beat off an enemy counter-attack. The face-slapping incident in Sicily is well known, and I mention it because, when I visited Patton on the day after it happened, he told me about it and asked my advice as we drove in his car to the front.

He said: 'I was going round the hospital where our boys were lying badly wounded, and I spoke to each of them and sympathized with them. And then I came to a bed where a young man was lying. I asked him about his wound, and he said: "I'm not wounded, sir —I just can't take it!"' On which Patton said, according to his own account: 'You can't take it! And you hide here among your wounded comrades!' And after slapping the man in the face with his gloves he turned to the medical officer and gave the order: 'Send him back to the front.'

General Patton was very worried and asked me for my advice. I said, 'George, this is a family affair—I can't give you any advice. You must ask General Eisenhower.' General Ike told him to apologize to the hospital—and he did so.

I think I am right in saying that the Press was asked not to report the incident. If the story got into the papers America's best fighting general would have to be relieved of his command because of public opinion at home. A certain American columnist got hold of the story and published it—and General Patton did lose his command. Otherwise he would, I presume, have commanded the U.S. Fifth Army in Italy in place of General Mark Clark.

In spite of all his bravura and toughness and terrific drive General Georgie Patton was a very emotional man. He loved his men and they loved him. I have been with him at the front when he was greeted with demonstrations of affection by his soldiers; and there were—as I saw for myself—tears running down his cheeks. He was a very rich man, and had been a fine athlete in his youth, having represented the United States in the Olympic Games at Stockholm in 1912, in the modern Pentathlon. Patton had very strict moral principles, and he once told me how wrong and unwise it was for a soldier of high standing to have any intimate association with women during war-time. Withal, he was of course a bit of a poseur. During the planning for the invasion of Sicily I asked him if he was satisfied with the plans for his Seventh Army. He clicked

45

his heels, saluted, and said: 'General, I don't plan—I only obey orders.' As a matter of fact, this was a reassuring remark, because I knew that he took the utmost care and interest in the planning side of his operations.

In short, a great character and a fine, aggressive, fighting commander who showed his ability in the conquest of Sicily and even more in his drive to the Rhine in 1944-5.

BATTLE MAPS

The Desert

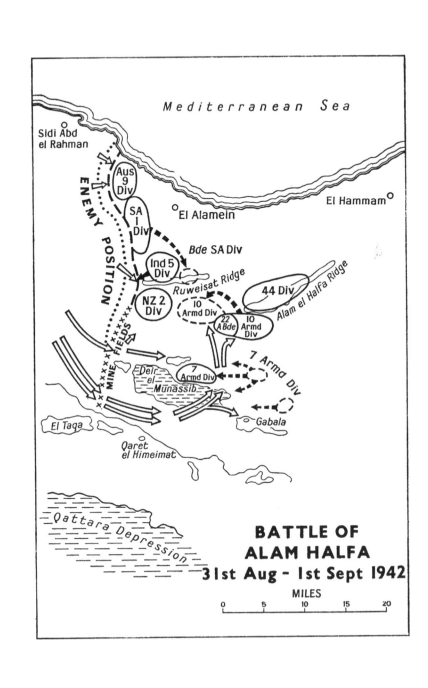

Mediterranean Sea

Sidi Abd
el Rahman

El Hammam

Aus 9 Div

SA 1 Div

El Alamein

ENEMY POSITION

Bde SA Div

Ind 5 Div

Ruweisat Ridge

44 Div

NZ 2 Div

10 Armd Div

Alam el Halfa Ridge

22 A Bde

10 Armd Div

MINE FIELDS

7 Armd Div

Deir el Munassib

7 Armd Div

El Taqa

Gabala

Qaret el Himeimat

Qattara Depression

**BATTLE OF
ALAM HALFA
31st Aug - 1st Sept 1942**

MILES

0   5   10   15   20

The Desert

The fighting in the Western Desert between the Axis and the British and Imperial forces had fluctuated between Benghazi and Tobruk since December 1940. By July 1942 Eighth Army was again back on Egyptian soil, standing at bay on the Alamein position only sixty miles west of Alexandria. On 15 August I formally succeeded to the Middle East Command, with orders to destroy the Axis forces in North Africa. Montgomery had taken over command of Eighth Army on 13 August, the anniversary of the battle of Blenheim, 1704. Winston Churchill, then in Cairo, was not unmindful of it. On that day, in a personal message, he wrote: 'May the anniversary of Blenheim that marks the opening of the new Command bring to the Commander of the Eighth Army and his troops the fame and fortune they will surely deserve.' Reinforcements were now arriving; and it was shortly to become possible to form an armoured corps—X Armoured Corps, comprising 1, 8 and 10 Armoured Divisions. A new phase in the desert campaign against Rommel's Panzerarmee was about to begin.

BATTLE OF ALAM HALFA
31 August–1 September 1942

For defensive purposes the Alamein position was geographically strong. Its right rested directly on the sea; its left—less directly—on the impassable Qattara Depression. Rommel, still riding high on the tide of success—he had repulsed the last attack of the old Eighth Army as recently as 27 July—was already planning an offensive that would carry him to the Nile Delta and to Cairo. Eighth Army's own preparations for an offensive were still only in the organizational stage. Montgomery therefore planned a purely defensive battle.

As anticipated, Rommel attacked with his armour round the left

49

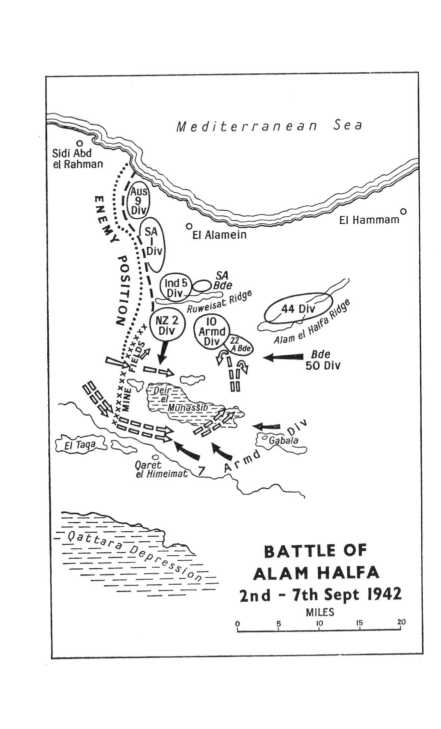

Mediterranean Sea

Sidi Abd
el Rahman

Aus
9
Div

SA
1
Div

El Alamein

El Hammam

Ind 5
Div

SA
Bde

Ruweisat Ridge

44 Div

Alam el Halfa Ridge

NZ 2
Div

10
Armd
Div

22
A Bde

Bde
50 Div

ENEMY POSITION

MINE FIELDS

Deir
el
Munassib

Gabala

Armd
Div

El Taqa

7

Qaret
el Himeimat

Qattara Depression

**BATTLE OF
ALAM HALFA
2nd - 7th Sept 1942**

MILES

0   5   10   15   20

flank, hoping to roll up Eighth Army from the south and to achieve its 'final annihilation'. The battle began in the early hours of 31 August, when enemy armoured columns penetrated the British minefields. 7 Armoured Division fell back before this onslaught, while light forces harassed the enemy's flanks. But when the enemy armour turned northwards behind the Eighth Army front, it was definitely held short of Alam el Halfa ridge, which was defended in strength by 22 Armoured Brigade and 44 Division. This disposal of strength resulted in severe loss to the German armour. Montgomery now ordered the redeployment of 10 Armoured Division between the ridge and New Zealand 2 Division on the main front.

Meanwhile frontal attacks had been made against Australian 9 Division, near the coast, and in the centre, held by South African 1 Division and Indian 5 Division. The coastal attack achieved nothing; the attack in the centre, made by an Italian division, secured a footing on the western end of Ruweisat Ridge, whence it dislodged by counter-attack by the end of the first day. A little farther south, the German 90 Light Division drove through the British minefields north of Deir el Munassib—a minor depression—and was less easily to be dislodged.

On 1 September renewed efforts of the enemy armoured forces west of Ruweisat failed with heavy loss and the German columns eventually disengaged. The Desert Air Force had played an important role in the battle throughout the day; and, in particular, its bombing of Tobruk had killed Rommel's hope of quick re-supply: a key factor in his decision to call off the attack.

BATTLE OF ALAM HALFA
2–7 September 1942

The enemy attempted little on 2 September, when he continued to be harassed by the light forces of 7 Armoured Division and was still suffering from the attacks of the Desert Air Force. On the fourth day—3 September—the enemy armour finally turned on its tracks. That night New Zealand 2 Division counter-attacked southwards and fighting continued in the Deir el Munassib during the next two days. When Montgomery called off the battle on the morning of 7 September, the enemy remained in possession of the western edge of the British minefields. Montgomery comments: 'It suited me to have their forces in strength on the southern flank since I was considering making my main blow, later on, on the northern part of the front.'

Eighth Army was now free to resume preparations for its own offensive. Winston Churchill pressed for it to be launched with the

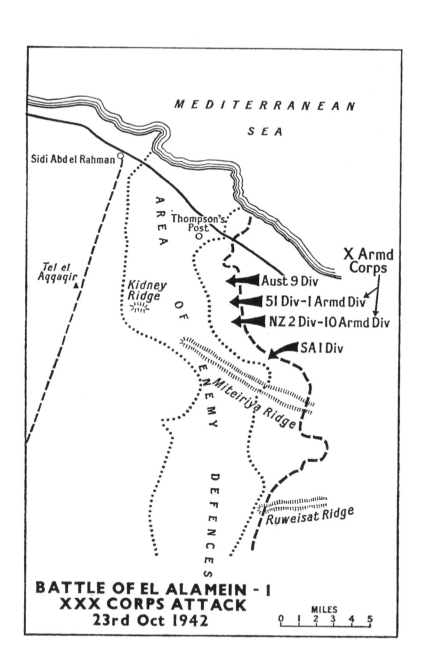

MEDITERRANEAN

SEA

Sidi Abd el Rahman

Thompson's Post

X Armd Corps

Tel el Aqqaqir

Kidney Ridge

← Aust 9 Div

← 51 Div - I Armd Div

← NZ 2 Div - 10 Armd Div

SA I Div

AREA OF ENEMY DEFENCES

Miteiriya Ridge

Ruweisat Ridge

BATTLE OF EL ALAMEIN - I
XXX CORPS ATTACK
23rd Oct 1942

MILES
0 1 2 3 4 5

least possible delay. On 17 September he reminded me: 'My under-standing with you was the fourth week in September.' But Alam Halfa had since intervened, and I replied firmly: 'I have carefully considered the timing in relation to "Torch" [the North African landings at the other end of the Mediterranean at that time fixed for 4 November] and have come to the conclusion that the best date for us to start would be minus 13 of "Torch".' The Prime Minister replied: 'We are in your hands.'

BATTLE OF EL ALAMEIN, XXX CORPS ATTACK
23 October 1942

The Eighth Army in the Alamein position was faced by Axis forces in occupation of an area well organized for defence. From the sea deep into the desert, a belt of minefields and defended localities extended to a depth of four miles or more. The enemy's flanks were secure. Under conditions of static warfare, the anti-tank gun screen had provided the answer to the tank assault; and there was now no alternative to a frontal infantry attack to 'blow a hole' in the enemy defences to enable British armour to break through into the open desert beyond.

The preparations for the forthcoming 'set-piece' battle could not altogether be concealed; and for this reason I attached very great importance to the deceptive measures to be taken to conceal our intentions as to the exact date and place of the attack. The deception plan—based on dummy tanks, guns, transport, dumps, pipelines—showed from the air concentrations of troops and administrative preparations in the southern XIII Corps sector large enough to suggest a full-scale attack, but incomplete—in order to suggest a later date than the actual. In the northern XXX Corps sector, calculations were made to determine what the area would look like from the air immediately before the battle. This picture had been reproduced on the ground by 1 October: at a later date the guns and the limbers were moved in by night and concealed under the dum-mies. Again, when 10 Armoured Corps, lying behind XXX Corps, moved from its training area to two staging areas four days before the battle opened, these moves were carried out openly as training moves. Thereafter the tanks and the guns moved to their assembly areas entirely by night—dummy tanks and vehicles immediately replacing them in their old locations.

The preliminary bombardment by over a thousand pieces of artillery was augmented by the bombers of the Desert Air Force; and on the night of 23–24 October four infantry divisions attacked north of Miteiriya Ridge—between Ruweisat and the sea—with the

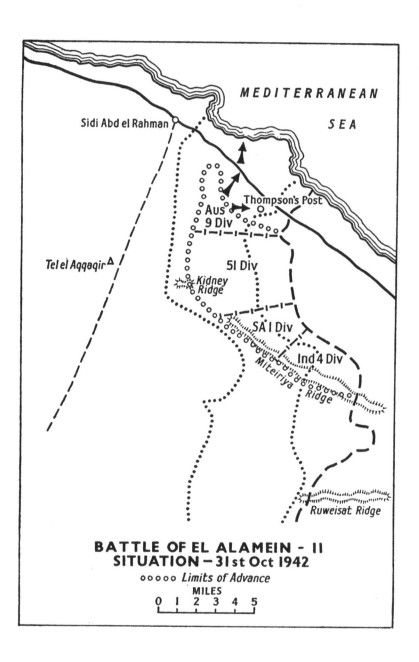

MEDITERRANEAN

SEA

Sidi Abd el Rahman

Thompson's Post

Aus
9 Div

Tel el Aqqaqir △

51 Div

Kidney
Ridge

SA I Div

Ind 4 Div

Miteiriya
Ridge

Ruweisat Ridge

**BATTLE OF EL ALAMEIN - II
SITUATION – 31st Oct 1942**

ooooo *Limits of Advance*

MILES

0 1 2 3 4 5

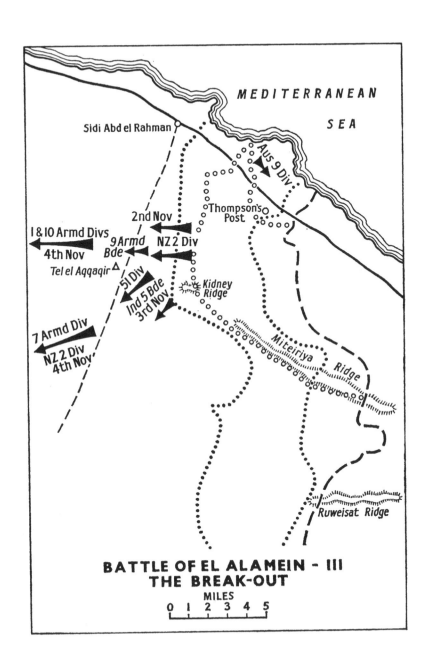

MEDITERRANEAN

SEA

Sidi Abd el Rahman

Aus 9 Div

Thompson's
Post

2nd Nov

1 & 10 Armd Divs

4th Nov

9 Armd
Bde

NZ 2 Div

Tel el Aqqaqir △

51 Div

Ind 5 Bde
3rd Nov

Kidney
Ridge

7 Armd Div

NZ 2 Div
4th Nov

Miteiriya   Ridge

Ruweisat Ridge

BATTLE OF EL ALAMEIN – III
THE BREAK-OUT

MILES

0   1   2   3   4   5

task of clearing two corridors through the enemy position. By the morning of the 24th, after hard fighting, the assaulting infantry of XXX Corps had bitten deeply into the defences; but the way was not yet clear for the armour to pass through and gain freedom of. manoeuvre.

The 'dog-fight' continued through the following days; the infantry improved their positions; and the first of the British armour got into action, but was severely hampered in its movements by the German anti-tank defence screen. On the other hand, counter-attacks against the area of the break-in caused the Afrika Korps heavy losses in tanks; and the full armoured battle could not now be long delayed.

BATTLE OF EL ALAMEIN
Situation 31 October 1942

To the north Australian 9 Division had attacked towards the coast with considerable success, thereby attracting to that quarter strong German forces to protect the coast road, the enemy's principal line of communication.

Although XIII Corps, south of Ruweisat Ridge, was active, its gains had been limited by minefields and anti-tank gun fire; but it was no part of Montgomery's plan that the corps should be deeply committed. Thus, by the end of the month, British armour had yet to gain the open desert.

BATTLE OF EL ALAMEIN, THE BREAK-OUT

Montgomery had been engaged in regrouping his forces and preparing to give to the offensive the fresh impetus it needed. Now, with some variation of the point of attack, he decided to go all out for the break-through: an effort that could never have succeeded but for the hammering the enemy had already sustained.

The Australians were still fighting in the coastal area when, at one in the morning of 2 November, a force under New Zealand command broke the enemy defences in the centre of the original frontage of attack and thereby enabled 9 Armoured Brigade to break through to the west. On 3 November a penetration to the south-west by 23 Armoured Brigade completed the operation. By the morning of 4 November, British 1, 7, and 10 Armoured Divisions were freely operating in the open desert, some miles beyond the original minefield area; the Axis forces were disintegrating; the Afrika Korps itself was in full retreat. Within the space of a few hours, the long attrition of Alamein had suddenly ceased to be a battle; the problem was now one of pursuit.

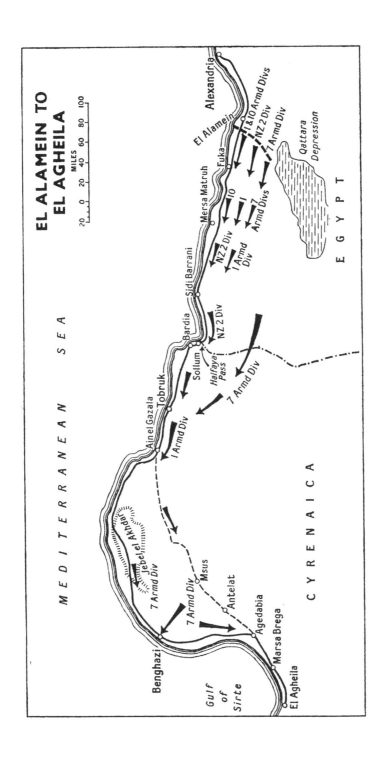

EL ALAMEIN TO EL AGHEILA

With the enemy in full retreat, the aim of Eighth Army was to cut off the Axis forces streaming westward along the coast road. British XIII Corps, to the south, moved quickly to round up the Italian divisions—in whose fate the Afrika Korps betrayed singular unconcern. British armour swung northwards to cut the coast road at Fuka and Mersa Matruh—respectively sixty and 110 miles west of Alamein. But now the weather intervened. Heavy rain on 6 and 7 November bogged down the advanced troops of Eighth Army— which was faced by a desert passage, whereas the Afrika Korps was able to conduct its retreat by road. Thus there developed the stern chase that was to continue to El Agheila.

In the pursuit the Desert Air Force, as a long-range weapon, was a key factor. As the advance continued, not only did it strike at the enemy's communications, but it secured along the coast of Cyrenaica a series of bases from which protection could be extended to the perilous Malta supply convoys.

Hardly less urgent was the problem of transport and supply both for Eighth Army and for the Desert Air Force. The long haul from Egypt needed to be eliminated at the earliest possible moment: the spearhead of Eighth Army's advance was governed by the number of fighting troops it could maintain. The answer to this administrative problem lay in the early capture of three Mediterranean ports: Tobruk, Benghazi, and, eventually, Tripoli. The British and American landings at Casablanca, Oran, and Algiers at this juncture, designed to ensure the quick capture of Bizerta and Tunis, were to prove abortive; and the whole future of the North African campaign still rested with the swift progress of Eighth Army.

The pursuit got going again at dawn on 8 November; and, on the 11th, 7 Armoured Division crossed the frontier of Cyrenaica— after covering 160 miles in three days along the escarpment—to be followed the next day by the New Zealand 2 Division. On the 13th Tobruk was entered by 22 Armoured Brigade—the star brigade of Alam Halfa. After traversing the hill mass of Jebel el Aldidar, 7 Armoured Division occupied Benghazi a week later; and, cutting straight across the desert, reached the shores of the Gulf of Sirte, near Agedabia. A turning movement persuaded the enemy to withdraw from the town; but it speedily became obvious that he was prepared to stand at El Agheila, where the rough and broken nature of the country favoured the defence. Earlier on in the North African campaign Eighth Army had twice reached El Agheila—only to withdraw. This time there was to be no going back.

58

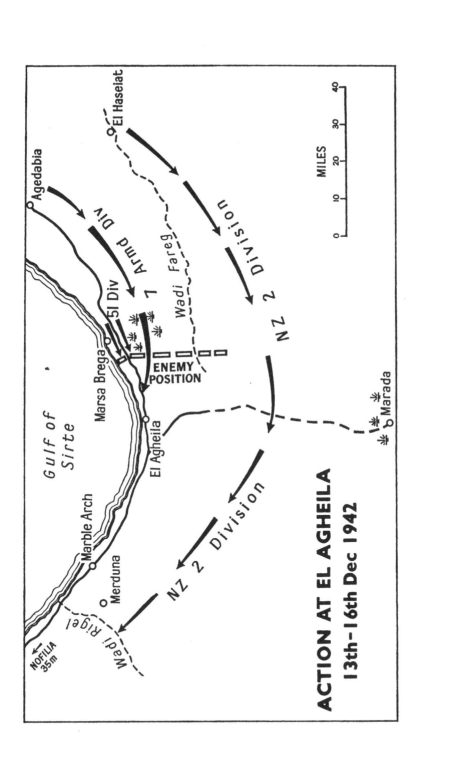

ACTION AT EL AGHEILA
13th–16th Dec 1942

ACTION AT EL AGHEILA
13–16 December 1942

Time was required for Eighth Army to stage an attack upon the Agheila position. Fortunately the port of Tobruk was soon in working order; but supplies had still to be accumulated and additional troops were necessary for the forthcoming operation.

When the attack finally went in, on 13 December, after an air and artillery bombardment the day before, the enemy had already decided to withdraw. In spite of minefields and other obstacles, he was followed up closely by 51 Highland Division on the coast road and by 7 Armoured Division to the left of it. To the south New Zealand 2 Division undertook a wide flanking movement and made good progress; but the Germans, split now into small detachments, fought desperately to withdraw in good order, though at heavy cost to themselves. By 16 December they were again in full retreat; and on the 18th, the New Zealanders, in a last effort to intercept them, fought a brisk engagement at Nofilia.

The battle had been won, and ill-omened Agheila, thankfully, had slipped into history; but Eighth Army was now in danger of outrunning its supplies, and contact with the enemy could be maintained only by light forces.

ACTION AT BUERAT AND ADVANCE TO TRIPOLI
15–23 January 1943

The enemy retreated rapidly after breaking away from Agheila; but there could be little doubt that Rommel was receiving substantial reinforcements through Tripoli and soon would stand and fight again. He chose a position beyond Buerat, where several deep wadis favoured the defence.

It was Montgomery's intention, once the enemy was dislodged from the Buerat position, to advance without pause, and with the utmost speed, on Tripoli. The build-up for the operation was dependent on quick supply through Benghazi; but heavy storms did great damage to the port and sunk several ships in the first week of January 1943, and the build-up was delayed by a reversion to the long haul from Tobruk. Since the time factor was all-important, Montgomery solved the maintenance problem by attacking with smaller forces than originally planned. 51 Division would press the advance along the coast, while 7 Armoured Division and New Zealand 2 Division would sweep round the enemy's southern flank.

The southern column moved on the morning of 15 January, and

made good progress, destroying a number of enemy tanks; and when, that night, 51 Division went in, the enemy was already in retreat. By next morning the southern column was round Rommel's right flank; near the coast the advance continued to go well; and between these two thrusts 22 Armoured Brigade was directed to Bir Dufan. But now movement on the battlefield began to slow down because of the ever-present minefields and skilful demolitions; while in the desert itself the 'going' was desperately difficult. Nevertheless, largely as the result of personal pressure from the Army Commander, by 19 January British forces were in Homs on the coast and the southern column was threatening Tarhuna; and the Desert Air Force was striking hard and often at an enemy now again in retreat. But the pace was still too slow; and 23 Armoured Brigade was put into the lead on the coast road beyond Homs with orders to force its way through Castelverde and continue to Tripoli.

This final stage of the advance was maintained by day and by night. So thorough were the demolitions that infantry had to be rushed forward to assist the tanks in their efforts to surmount them. Meanwhile the southern column had passed Tarhuna and was now also heading for Tripoli—with the enemy rearguards in flight to the west. On 23 January, Tripoli was entered from the east and from the south—while the unresting 7 Armoured Division still pushed ahead to keep contact with the enemy, by way of Zuara, where it fought a minor engagement. On 3 February, the first supply ship discharged at the restored port of Tripoli; and Eighth Army, its maintenance now assured, was able to prepare for the invasion of Tunisia. Four 'set-piece' battles still lay ahead of Eighth Army; but it was at this point in time that the Eighteenth Army Group came into existence, comprising all the land forces in North Africa—British, American, and French—under my command. My first task was to reorganize the forces facing eastwards in Tunisia—the British First Army and the United States II Corps.

PURSUIT TO AND BATTLE OF MEDENINE

After the capture of Tripoli and the subsequent advance to the frontier of Tunisia, Eighth Army had completed the conquest of Italian North Africa; but, because of the weather and the action of enemy rearguards, the frontier was not crossed until February. By the middle of the month the village of Ben Gardane had been secured, and a few days later advanced troops had entered Medenine and Foum Tatahonine. Away on the southern flank a column of French troops under General Leclercq brilliantly concluded its long march from Lake Chad to join Eighth Army. It was directed to

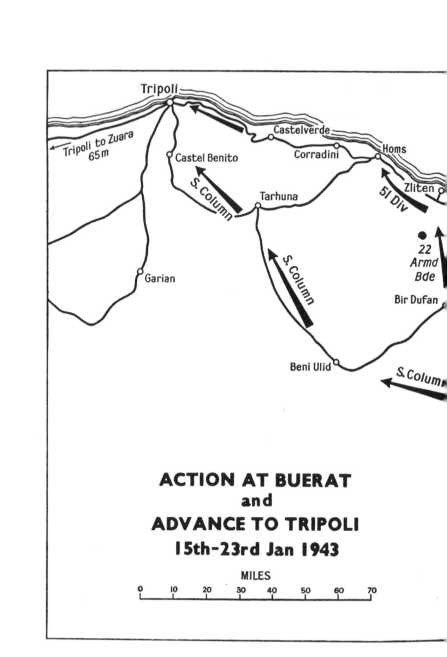

Tripoli

Tripoli to Zuara
65 m

Castel Benito

Castelverde

Corradini

Homs

Zliten

S. Column

Tarhuna

51 Div

S. Column

22
Armd
Bde

Garian

Bir Dufan

Beni Ulid

S. Column

ACTION AT BUERAT
and
ADVANCE TO TRIPOLI
15th-23rd Jan 1943

MILES

| 0 | 10 | 20 | 30 | 40 | 50 | 60 | 70 |

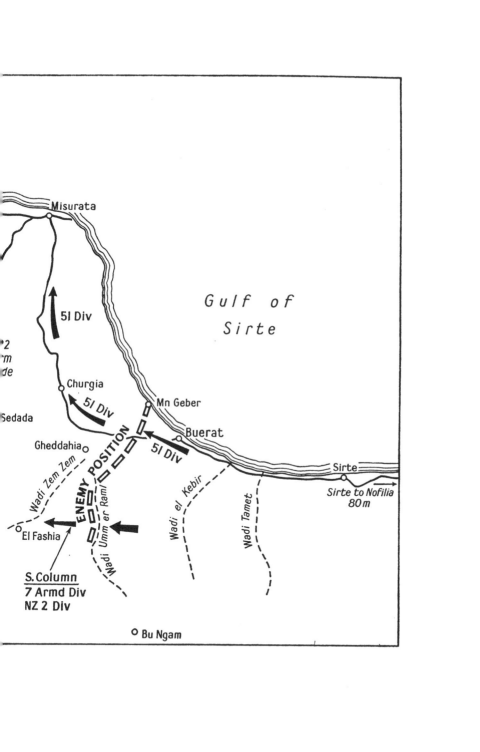

Misurata

Gulf of Sirte

51 Div

Churgia

51 Div

Mn Geber

Sedada

Buerat

51 Div

Gheddahia

Wadi Zem Zem

ENEMY POSITION

Wadi Umm er Raml

Wadi el Kebir

Wadi Tamet

Sirte

Sirte to Nofilia
80 m

El Fashia

S. Column
7 Armd Div
NZ 2 Div

Bu Ngam

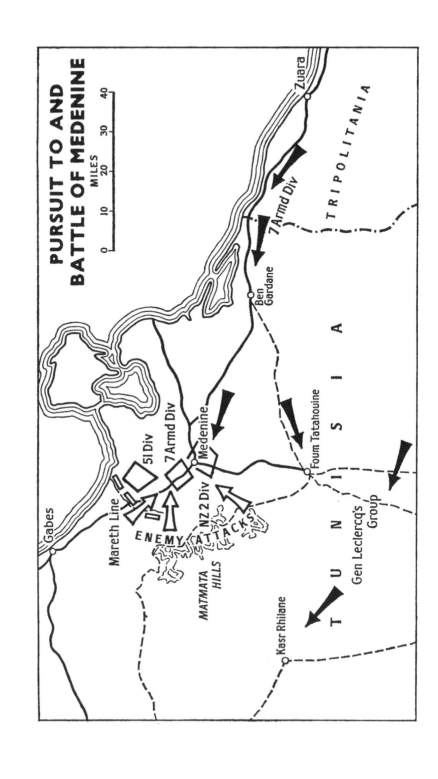

PURSUIT TO AND BATTLE OF MEDENINE

MILES

0 10 20 30 40

Zuara

TRIPOLITANIA

7 Armd Div

7 Armd Div

Ben Gardane

T U N I S I A

Foum Tatahouine

Gabes

Mareth Line

51 Div

7 Armd Div

Medenine

NZ 2 Div

ENEMY ATTACKS

MATMATA HILLS

Gen Leclercq's Group

Kasr Rhilane

advance north-westward on Kasr Rhilane. Eighth Army itself now regrouped and built up supplies for its attack on the Mareth Line— a line of fortifications originally constructed by the French as a frontier defence against Italian Libya and since made even more formidable under German direction.

On 15 February the Germans took the initiative on the other Tunisian frontier. They attacked United States II Corps in the southern sector and made such headway towards Tebessa that Allied positions farther north were endangered. I therefore urged Montgomery to exert all possible pressure in order to divert the enemy's attentions to the Eighth Army front. Its leading divisions— 7 Armoured and 51 Highland—at once stepped up their operations against the outer defences covering the Mareth Line—with the result that the German drive on Tebessa turned into retreat before the end of February. Eighth Army now found itself facing a reinforced enemy. Indeed, by 5 March Rommel had three armoured divisions in the region of the Matmata Hills; and signs were evident that, even at this late hour in the North African campaign, he was contemplating a second—and last—offensive against the new Eighth Army. A probing attack against British infantry near the coast proved ineffectual; and when, on 6 March, a concentrated advance of three armoured columns was directed on the northern side of Medenine, their progress was halted by 7 Armoured Division. Anti-tank gun fire decided the day. No more was Rommel to go a-roving. After making four main attacks with no success whatsoever, he drew off as darkness fell. For a change, all the tanks abandoned on the field were his own—fifty-two.

BATTLE OF MARETH

The fortifications of the coastal portion of the Mareth Line took full advantage of deep Wadi Zigzaou and offered no opportunity for a tank attack. The right rested on the mass of the Matmata Hills—the assumption being that the hills were difficult enough to prevent an outflanking movement. Westward of the hills stretched waterless desert.

Nevertheless Montgomery's plan for ejecting the Germans from the Mareth Line included a 'left hook' through the hills, combined with a heavy frontal assault against the coastal sector which, even if it could not hope for a break-through, would serve to detain strong enemy forces in this sector while the flanking movement took effect. In order to prevent the reinforcement of the German defenders, I arranged that the United States II Corps should attack towards Gafsa on 17 March.

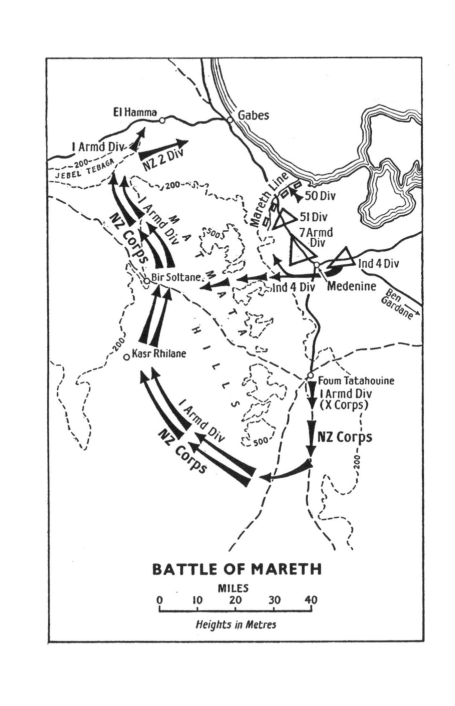

El Hamma

Gabes

I Armd Div

NZ 2 Div

JEBEL TEBAGA

200

200

Mareth Line

50 Div

I Armd Div

M A T M A T A

51 Div

7 Armd Div

500

NZ Corps

Bir Soltane

Ind 4 Div

Ind 4 Div

Medenine

Ben Gardane

200

H I L L S

Kasr Rhilane

Foum Tatahouine

I Armd Div (X Corps)

500

NZ Corps

I Armd Div

NZ Corps

200

BATTLE OF MARETH

MILES

0   10   20   30   40

Heights in Metres

Montgomery's outflanking column consisted of New Zealand 2 Division augmented to the strength and style of a corps by the addition of 8 Armoured Brigade, the French under General Leclercq, an armoured-car regiment, and a regiment of artillery. It set out on its hazardous march on 20 March. The services of bull-dozers and engineers were in constant need to keep the vehicles moving. First the column headed south; then, through a gap in the hills, north-westwards; finally northwards, passing by Kasr Rhilane and Bir Soltane. Before darkness fell on the 21st, the advance guard was approaching the defile in the hills south of Jebel Tebaga. It was strongly defended, but secured after a night attack—with a large haul of Italian prisoners.

50 Division delivered its frontal attack on the Mareth Line in the coastal sector on the first night of the battle. It gained footholds on the farther bank of Wadi Zigzaou against heavy opposition—shortly to be reinforced by the arrival of a German armoured division, which gained ground. Montgomery therefore decided to reinforce strongly his 'left hook' and to confine further effort in the coastal sector to the pinning down of the enemy. Thus, on the night of 23 March, 50 Division withdrew from the farther side of the Wadi; but, in common with the other divisions engaged in this sector—51 and 7 Armoured—maintained an active and threatening role. Meanwhile 1 Armoured Division had been despatched to join the New Zealand Corps to assist in the forcing of the Tebaga defile; and Indian 4 Division was brought forward from Medenine to open up a shorter line of advance through the hills to Bir Soltane.

The Tebaga defile was forced by an attack that began on the after-noon of 26 March, after the Desert Air Force had severely shaken its defenders. The New Zealand Corps led the march through the defile, with 1 Armoured Division hard on its heels. After a night pause for the moon to rise, by dawn 1 Armoured Division was out of the defile and approaching El Hamma. Farther east the New Zealanders were still heavily engaged; but by evening the victory was complete. Montgomery's stratagem had come off. On this same day—27 March—Indian 4 Division, after meeting some opposition, reached Bir Soltane.

When darkness fell on the 27th the Germans abandoned the Mareth Line in the coastal sector and retreated with all speed along the Gabes road. Close pursuit was ruled out by mines, booby traps, and demolitions; in the region of El Hamma dust storms hindered further movement; and beyond Gabes Eighth Army was still faced by yet one more defensive position—Wadi Akarit—before it could break into the Tunisian plain.

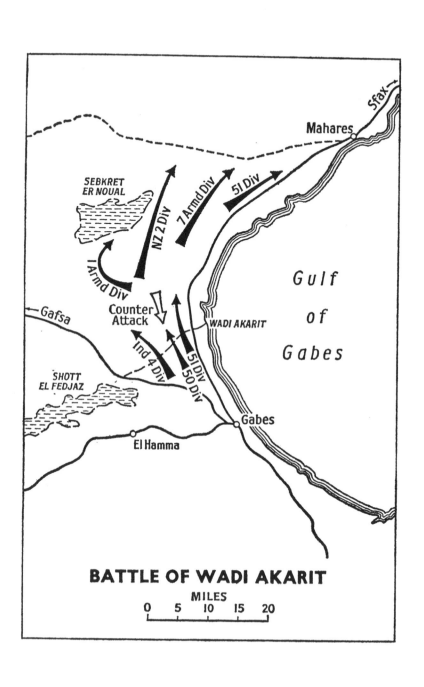

SEBKRET
ER NOUAL

NZ 2 Div

7 Armd Div

51 Div

Mahares

Sfax

Gulf
of
Gabes

1 Armd Div

Counter
Attack

WADI AKARIT

Gafsa

Ind 4 Div

51 Div
50 Div

SHOTT
EL FEDJAZ

Gabes

El Hamma

BATTLE OF WADI AKARIT

MILES

0   5   10   15   20

BATTLE OF WADI AKARIT

The enemy evacuated El Hamma on 29 March and the New Zealanders entered Gabes. The Axis forces now stood on Wadi Akarit, to the south of the Tunisian plain, which extends to Enfidaville. On this narrow front, between the coast and an expanse of water and marshland, their flanks were secure. Moreover, the landward end of the position was backed by hills that gave good observation.

Thus there was no opportunity for manoeuvre, and time was short. Eighth Army and the Desert Air Force were still drawing their supplies from Tripoli, some three hundred miles distant; the need for Sfax and Sousse as base ports was urgent. Once again the only solution was a powerful frontal attack—to force the enemy back into the open and to allow armour to sweep into the plain.

Three divisions of XXX Corps—50, 51, and Indian 4—were to deliver the assault. X Corps—1 Armoured, 7 Armoured, and New Zealand 2 Divisions—stood close in rear to await the moment of advance. The attack was launched in early darkness on 6 April. Two of the best German divisions delivered the expected counter-attacks. When night fell XXX Corps had not yet succeeded in breaking through; and X Corps began to move forward to add its weight to the battle. But before it was committed, pressure of British and Indian infantry had forced the enemy into retreat. By dawn of the 7th, XXX Corps was in pursuit along the coast road, with X Corps on its left.

Now only one more advance lay ahead of dauntless Eighth Army—and that to remain inconclusive. Not without a certain poignancy, 'the end in Africa' was not to crown its work unaided.

ADVANCE TO ENFIDAVILLE AND THE END IN AFRICA

Now the ring was beginning to close. Although German rearguards still offered resistance, mainly in the coastal areas, steady pressure was maintained on the enemy; and on 7 April, United States II Corps, advancing from Gafsa, made contact with X Corps on the Gabes road. British IX Corps, of First Army, had also started an offensive in the Fondouk area; and, by the 9th, 6 Armoured Division was advancing towards Kairouan.

Eighth Army, too, had quickened its progress. Sfax was entered on 10 April—five days ahead of schedule—and five days later XXX Corps captured Sousse. But already a basic decision was in sight—that First Army should make the main effort in the final phase of the campaign. An attack on Tunis and Bizerta could be more easily launched from the west; and a further advance by Eighth Army was

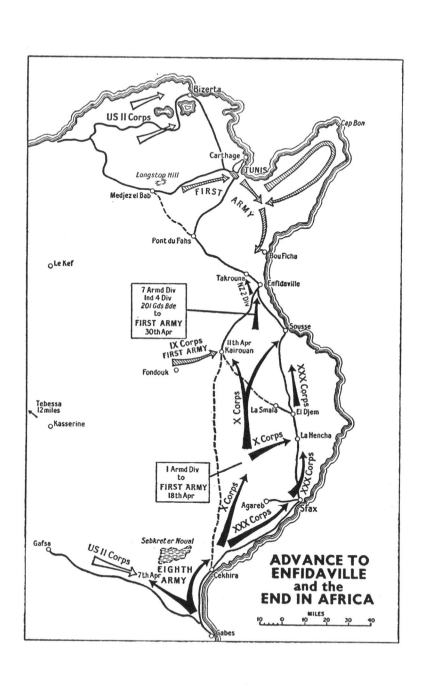

ADVANCE TO
ENFIDAVILLE
and the
END IN AFRICA

barred by the strong defensive position among the hills near Enfidaville. Its function henceforth would be to pin down the enemy strength on its front. At my request Montgomery released to First Army an armoured division and an armoured-car regiment— 1 Armoured Division and the King's Dragoon Guards.

Nevertheless Montgomery resolved to make a final test of the strength of the Enfidaville position. The task fell to X Corps, now comprising 7 Armoured, New Zealand 2, Indian 4, and 50 Divisions. The attack went in with full artillery and air support on the night of 19 April. It was to prove to be Eighth Army's last fling. After heavy fighting the inexhaustibly intrepid New Zealanders entered Takrouna and captured Enfidaville; but a succession of counter-attacks throughout the two following days persuaded the Army Commander that the cost of persevering with the offensive would be more than Eighth Army could afford. He had also to take count of Eighth Army's next assignment—the invasion of Sicily.

Now under my orders, First Army attacked in strength the German front in Tunisia to the north-west. It ran from the region of Pont du Fahs and Medjez el Bab, and thence northwards to cover Tunis and Bizerta on the west. But still there was no break-through, and at the end of the month I had to call upon Montgomery for additional and more powerful assistance. It was readily made available; and 7 Armoured and Indian 4 Divisions and 201 Guards Brigade, with some artillery, moved from Eighth Army to the First.

On 6 May First Army delivered the final successful blow. Next day the unfailing and ever-unflagging 7 Armoured Division led the advance into Tunis. Almost simultaneously, on that same day, American and French forces of the United States II Corps entered Bizerta. By 12 May all Axis resistance had ceased on the North African seaboard.

Two Defeats

VI

DUNKIRK

I HAVE told my story of victory in North Africa. Now I must chronicle two defeats—Dunkirk and Burma.

When the shooting war started in the spring of 1940, we advanced into Belgium and took up positions covering Brussels, unopposed by the enemy air. The willingness of the Germans to tolerate this forward movement, from our prepared positions on the Franco–Belgian frontier, was highly suspicious. But we know now, of course, that they must have welcomed it—by drawing us forward they could hope to encircle our southern flank.

I was commanding the British 1 Division, and on gaining contact with the advanced German elements I was not unduly pressed. However, when the enemy broke through the French on my right, I was forced to withdraw to avoid encirclement. The retreat to Dunkirk had already begun; and, although my own division was still not heavily attacked, I had to conform to the movements of the formations on my flanks in order to hold a united front. This general withdrawal soon developed into a situation of acute peril. The position of the B.E.F. was rather like that of a ripe pear hanging precariously on its branch at Dunkirk—then not only our main base but our port of entry into the continent of Europe.

We were completely surrounded except for the corridor to our base; and, as we withdrew into a smaller perimeter covering Dunkirk itself, the Germans continued to press their advantage, though not to the extent their strength permitted. If Hitler had thrown the full weight of his armies into destroying the B.E.F., it could never have escaped. If I am asked, '*Who* saved the B.E.F.?' my reply is 'Hitler.'

On the political side I have heard it said that Hitler was convinced that Britain would be prepared to come to terms once France—

'the continental soldier'—was eliminated; it might, therefore, be inopportune to humiliate Britain by capturing her army.

At Charleville, on 24 May, when the B.E.F. was absolutely ripe for the plucking, he informed his astonished generals that Britain was 'indispensable' to the world and that he had therefore resolved to respect her integrity and, if possible, ally himself with her. Perhaps a less fanciful explanation of Hitler's attitude is supplied by Ribbentrop's representative at the Führer's headquarters, who has left on record the comment: 'Hitler personally intervened to allow the British to escape. He was convinced that to destroy their army would be to force them to fight to the bitter end.'

On the military side the facts are clearer. On 23 May Field-Marshal von Rundstedt, commanding Army Group A, halted General Guderian's XIX Army Corps when two of its panzer divisions were heading for Dunkirk, not twenty miles distant and with little or no opposition ahead. The British counter-attack at Arras on 21 May, though undertaken by no more than two mixed columns, each comprising a tank battalion, an infantry battalion, a field battery, an anti-tank battery, and a machine-gun company, had caused him some concern. He therefore called the halt in order to 'allow the situation to clarify itself and keep our forces concentrated'. The panzers had just reached the Channel, and the success of this British counter-attack engendered the fear of a larger operation that would cut them off from their supporting infantry.

The next morning he received a visit from the Führer, who confirmed the stop order. The panzers were not to be risked in a possibly flooded area but preserved for future operations—presumably against the French Army. On the other hand, the Luftwaffe's 'field of action' was not to be restricted.

Actually, on the available evidence, there can be little doubt that it was at the particular instance of the Luftwaffe's commander-in-chief, Field-Marshal Göring, that in the upshot the B.E.F. was 'left to the Luftwaffe'. Guderian was to write, bitterly, of the first day of the evacuation, 26 May: 'We watched the Luftwaffe attack. We saw also the armada of great and little ships, by means of which the British were evacuating their forces.' Guderian's bitterness was shared by the whole of the German Army High Command; but Hitler's personal decision can hardly have derived from sheer military stupidity.

When he remarked that he did not propose to send the panzers into the marshes of Flanders—which he recalled from his own experiences in the winter of 1916–17—he added, 'We shall not hear much more of the British in this war'. In his view the B.E.F. at that time was a defeated rabble and would count for nothing in the foreseeable future.

Two months later—on 21 July—at the first full conference on the hastily drafted plans for invading England, he made clear his own attitude: 'Our attention must be turned to tackling the Russian problem.' Planning for it started immediately.

One may even doubt whether Hitler was ever seriously interested in the whole invasion project. In the recently published *The Testament of Adolf Hitler, February–April,* 1945,* the following entry appears: 'Even by the end of July, one month, that is, after the defeat of France, I realized that peace was once again eluding our grasp. A few weeks later I knew that we should not succeed in invading Britain before the advent of the autumnal gales because we had not succeeded in acquiring complete command of the air. In other words, I realized that we should never succeed in invading Britain.'

Thus the B.E.F. succeeded in withdrawing into a defensible perimeter around Dunkirk, from which we eventually succeeded in getting away all our soldiers though we lost all our heavy equipment.

General Sir Alan Brooke, who was the corps commander most concerned in stemming the German attacks, handled the situation in a most able manner; but I am of the opinion that our C.-in-C., Lord Gort, who had the over-all responsibility, has not received sufficient recognition for his conduct of the whole withdrawal operation.

The British front-line soldier, as always, showed a tough fighting spirit in retreat and could not have done more to save the situation. Yet I was not satisfied with the conduct of the rear administrative services, who were the first elements to be evacuated. When I reached the beaches with my division, I found the sands littered with personal weapons that had been thrown away—rifles, pistols, tommy-guns, and so on.

I myself reached the beaches on a pushbike after abandoning my car some miles back, because the roads were hopelessly blocked by French, Belgian, and British soldiers. The car was set alight in

* Cassell, 1961.

order that the Germans should not have the enjoyment of my personal belongings or the use of the vehicle itself. Thus my sole remaining possessions for the remainder of the battle were my revolver, my field glasses, and my brief case.

My divisional engineers drove their lorries on to the beaches at low tide and bridged them with a superstructure of planks to make a pier. Thus, when the tide came in, small rowing-boats could take off six or eight soldiers to small ships or other craft waiting to receive them. The plan was that every boat-load taken off would have someone detailed to row it back for the next consignment. I was not very pleased with the response.

However, to take a broader view of the whole proceedings, I realize that only a few handfuls of our troops could have been got off under these conditions. The great evacuation was done on the mole, where complete units were embarked on destroyers and corvettes which carried away thousands of men.

I believe, but I am not too sure, that when the troops were being evacuated the Navy demanded or advised that the men should come aboard unencumbered by their personal weapons. This may have been the reason why so many of them were left behind on the beaches. But I can say with some pride as a Guardsman that every battalion of the Foot Guards arrived back in England with their complement of personal weapons still intact. Nor is it a legend that their trousers were pressed!

As regards my own personal responsibility in the evacuation, at a fairly late stage—on 31 May—I was given the command of the rearguard and took over I Corps when General Lord Gort handed over the B.E.F. and was ordered back to England.

His verbal instructions to me were that it was officially understood that I should take my orders from the French Command and co-operate with them to the best of my ability. Since this directive seemed very unsatisfactory, I rang up the Secretary of State for War, Anthony Eden, whom I got on to from G.H.Q. at La Panne, a few miles to the east of Dunkirk. Incidentally, this was the last communication by telephone with England, as the line was then cut by the German advance.

I asked Eden what my orders were. He said: 'Take your orders from the French Command, unless you think they endanger the B.E.F.' I replied: 'The B.E.F. is already in extreme danger of being wiped out, and its only salvation is in immediate evacuation.' He said: 'I agree to immediate evacuation, but you must give the French 50-50 facilities with our own troops to get away.' To which I said: 'Right! I will do that.' And I did.

The French troops were given the same facilities as our own to go down to the mole at night and be taken off in Royal Navy vessels; but after a few nights the French quota fell far below our own, so I allocated one whole night for the evacuation of the French alone. But since no French soldiers turned up I realized I could do no more to help them, and we carried on evacuating the last of our own soldiers. I don't blame our French allies: as good Frenchmen they didn't want to leave France, but preferred to remain in their own country—even as prisoners of war.

Before the last night I sent my staff away. There was nothing heroic about this gesture: they were redundant, useless; there was nothing for them to do which I couldn't do myself, and they were valuable material for the future.

On the last night I toured the beaches with Admiral Bill Tennant in a small naval craft, to make sure that no one was left behind. Having satisfied myself that the whole of the rearguard had got safely away, I boarded a destroyer at the mole—which, incidentally, was receiving attention from spasmodic German machine-gun fire—and we set sail for England in the early morning of Monday, 3 June. It was a pleasant voyage, even if we were not ignored by the Luftwaffe, who bombed us unsuccessfully.

It should be apparent that I recall the whole affair of Dunkirk with extreme distaste: and there still lay ahead the bitter pill of Burma. Meanwhile I was happy to get down to the real business of war— or, rather, training for war—at Southern Command.

'BROOKIE'

General Sir Alan Brooke (now Field-Marshal Lord Alanbrooke) succeeded General Sir John Dill as Chief of the Imperial General Staff in December 1941. In his appointment the Prime Minister made a wise choice. I served under him as a commander in the field for most of the war and I could not have had a wiser, firmer, or more understanding military chief to guide and look after our interests. Brookie, as we always call him, was the outstanding and obvious man for the job; a fine soldier in every sense, and trusted and admired by the whole Army. He had proved himself a capable commander of a corps in the early days of the war, and had been a senior instructor at the Staff College before the war; he was therefore well equipped to shoulder the responsibilities of his high appointment.

Furthermore, he had a broader military background than other competitors for the post of C.I.G.S. He had served with the Canadians during the First World War, and, having been educated in France, he spoke French like a Frenchman, besides having a very workable knowledge of German. He understood the Americans, with whom he got on well, especially with General Marshall, who became his very good friend.

A man of strong character, Brookie was able to serve his great chief in the best possible way. Whether he relished his appointment as C.I.G.S. or whether he would have preferred to have an active command in the field, I do not know, but I suspect that he would have preferred high command. However, his appointment was welcomed by the Army and especially by those who knew him personally.

His family and mine have been friends and neighbours in Northern Ireland for many generations. The Brookes of Brookeborough and the Alexanders of Caledon are separated only by the length of the Clogher Valley, through which once ran the famous light railway whose engines we as boys drove in the old privileged days.

Now both have gone—those privileged days and the Clogher Valley Railway—much to our regret but perhaps to the relief of its shareholders and the taxpayers, not to mention the dogs, chickens, and frightened horses it daily put to flight on its career through the countryside. Today Brookie is the senior of our five Ulster Field-Marshals—and long may he live to enjoy that distinction.

Among my memories of him is an episode that occurred in 1941, when I had taken over Southern Command. Brookie held a largescale invasion exercise in which I was the commander of the anti-invasion forces. The exercise, the codename of which was 'Bumper', lasted several days and at the end I had destroyed the invader.

The conference on the exercise was held at the Staff College a few days later, and I expected to be given credit for my handling of the operations. However, I was disappointed to be severely criticized by the C.I.G.S., the director of the exercise, for not having moved my mass of manoeuvre to my left flank earlier. Since I had been given a deadline over which they were not allowed to cross before a certain time I felt that this was an unfair criticism.

I felt moved to get up in the conference and defend my action— and then I remembered a story that had impressed itself on my mind many years before. When I was General Sir Francis Gathorne-Hardy's chief of staff, he told me that, when he was a young captain in the Grenadiers, he went to the Kaiser's grand manoeuvres, where he was attached to a certain high-ranking German general. At the close of the manoeuvres his general was quite unfairly criticized for some action he had taken, or failed to take. When the conference on the exercise was over, Gathorne-Hardy, who rightly resented the criticism directed at his general, said to him: 'But, General, why didn't you get up and point to the error in the director's criticism?'

The general looked at Gathorne-Hardy severely and said: 'Young man, to criticize the Commander-in-Chief before the Army would be a death blow to the whole of German military discipline!'

There is sound reason for this acceptance of criticism in the conduct of exercises. The director will have designed his manoeuvres to bring out certain lessons—lessons of great value to all those taking part; and it would be a poor act for one individual, in defence of his own dignity, to destroy the value of the main lesson. That is why I have never expressed any resentment at being quite unfairly criticized during 'Bumper'.

BATTLE MAPS

Dunkirk

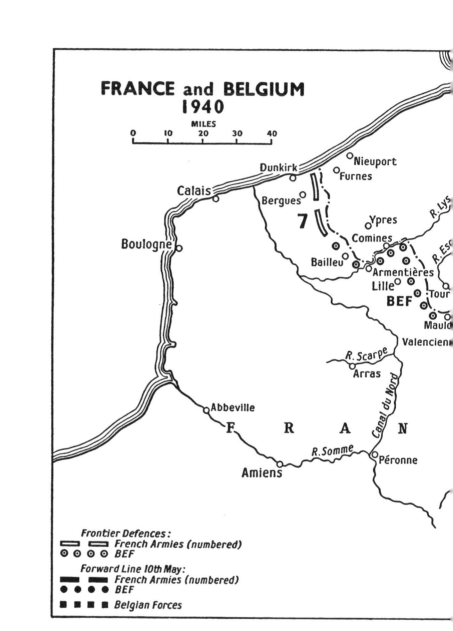

FRANCE and BELGIUM
1940

MILES

0   10   20   30   40

Nieuport
Furnes
Dunkirk
Bergues
Calais
Ypres
R. Lys
7
Comines
Boulogne
Bailleu
Armentières
Lille
Tour
BEF
Mauld
Valencien
R. Scarpe
Arras
Canal du Nord
Abbeville
F   R   A   N
R. Somme
Péronne
Amiens
R. Esc

Frontier Defences:
French Armies (numbered)
◉ ◉ ◉ ◉ BEF
Forward Line 10th May:
French Armies (numbered)
● ● ● ● BEF
■ ■ ■ ■ Belgian Forces

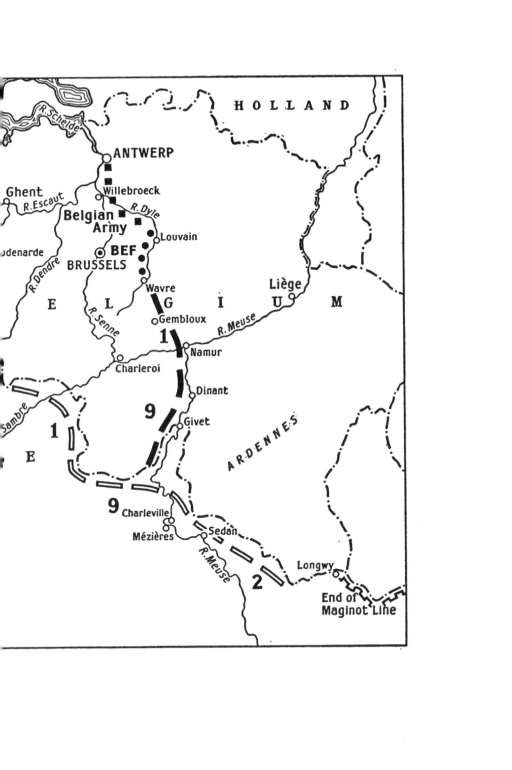

Dunkirk

A WEEK after the outbreak of war, 3 September 1939, the British Expeditionary Force began to cross the Channel to join the armies of France who were standing on the defensive along France's 'guarantee' against invasion from Germany—the Maginot Line. To the north it ended at Longwy; and from Longwy to the sea the French frontier marched with that of Belgium, still a neutral country.

FRANCE AND BELGIUM
1940

The B.E.F., in which I was commanding 1 Division, came into the French line along the Belgian border, taking over the sector between Maulde and Bailleul. Here, throughout the winter, the B.E.F. worked on the defences and trained for battle.

In November 1939 an agreement was concluded with Belgium whereby, if Belgium were invaded, the British and the French were to advance and take up their dispositions on Belgian soil, with their right along the Meuse to Namur and their left covering Brussels. The B.E.F. itself would be on the line of the River Dyle, from Wavre to Louvain, whence Belgian forces would hold the front northwards to Antwerp.

When, on 10 May 1940, after airborne descents and bombing attacks on Holland and Belgium, the Germans launched their invasion of the west, the Allies at once moved into Belgium—the B.E.F. taking up their positions on the Dyle, with French First Army on its right. To the south French Ninth Army was soon to be confronted by German armoured columns advancing through the 'impassable' Ardennes. By 13 May these columns had reached the Meuse, crossed it near Sedan and at Dinant, and continued their

86

swift advance after routing Ninth Army. Meanwhile, in Holland, the Dutch had offered little resistance to the German onslaught; by 15 May fighting had ceased. A retirement on the whole front was already in sight. The B.E.F. itself was shortly to be compelled to undertake a withdrawal—soon to culminate in the retreat to Dunkirk.

RETREAT TO DUNKIRK
May 1940

The B.E.F. repulsed the enemy at Wavre and Louvain and held on to its river-line; but when French First Army, its right flank now exposed, was obliged to draw back, Gort, the British Commander-in-Chief, arranged with the French Command for a withdrawal by stages to the Escaut—the Belgians on the left to conform. The movement began on 16 May. The first brief pause was on the River Senne, behind Brussels. By the 18th the Dendre had been reached; by the next day, after but little fighting, the B.E.F. was back on the Escaut, standing between Maulde and Audenarde. Already the German armoured columns, after crossing the old Somme battlefields, had reached Amiens and Abbeville, thus severing the communications of the B.E.F. Thence they turned northward to the coast.

The Allied forces now operating in Flanders and the French armies to the south were unable to co-ordinate proposals to attack the enemy's flanks from north and south: the solitary—and successful—British counter-attack that went in was at Arras, on 21 May. A further retirement was now inevitable, and on the night of the 22nd the B.E.F. left the Escaut, falling back on the frontier defences east of Lille and as far to the north-west as the River Lys, where Belgian troops held the front. On its other flank, French First Army fought on south of Lille. To meet the danger from the west, such troops as were available were allocated to the defence of the line of Canals running south-eastward from Gravelines to La Bassée.

The decision to evacuate the B.E.F. and embark it for England was taken on 25 May. This same day Boulogne fell to the Germans: Calais the day following. The Belgian Army, after relinquishing the line of the Lys, capitulated on 28 May; and the British had now to fill a gap on their left flank that extended towards Nieuport. Against increasing German pressure they could not hope to hold the canal line for long.

The B.E.F., which had fought a fighting retreat as far as the Lys, now headed with all speed for Dunkirk, where a defensive perimeter had been prepared, together with those troops of French First Army who had not been cut off in the neighbourhood of Lille.

87

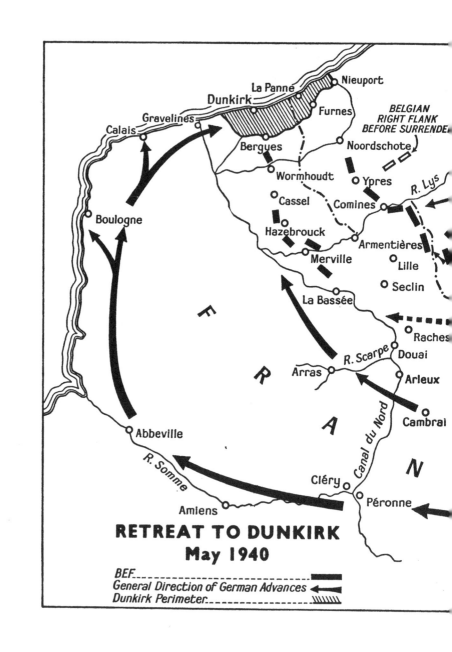

Nieuport
La Panné
Dunkirk
Furnes
Gravelines
Calais
Bergues
BELGIAN
RIGHT FLANK
BEFORE SURRENDER
Noordschote
Boulogne
Wormhoudt
Ypres
R. Lys
Cassel
Comines
Hazebrouck
Armentières
Merville
Lille
Seclin
F
La Bassée
R
R. Scarpe
Douai
Raches
Arras
Arleux
A
Canal du Nord
Cambrai
Abbeville
R. Somme
N
Cléry
Péronne
Amiens

RETREAT TO DUNKIRK
May 1940

BEF
General Direction of German Advances
Dunkirk Perimeter

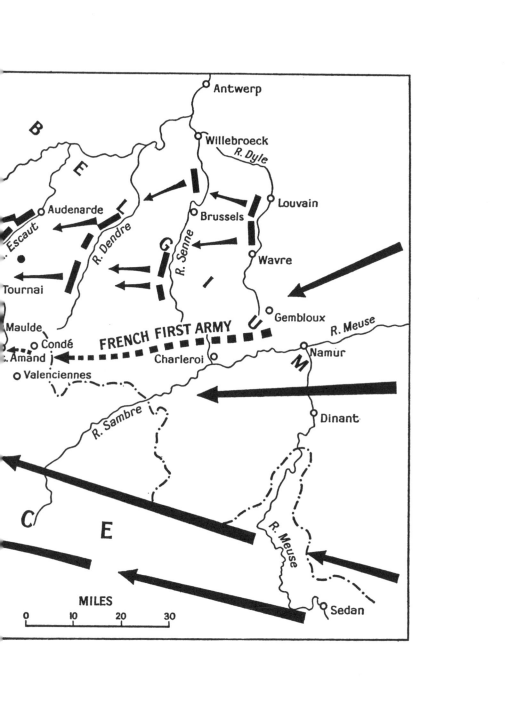

Antwerp

B

E

Willebroeck

R. Dyle

Audenarde

Escaut

R. Dendre

G

R. Senne

Brussels

Louvain

Wavre

I

Tournai

Maulde

Condé

Gembloux

R. Meuse

U

FRENCH FIRST ARMY

Amand

Charleroi

Namur

M

Valenciennes

R. Sambre

Dinant

C

E

R. Meuse

R. Meuse

Sedan

MILES

0   10   20   30

By 30 May nearly all the Allied forces due for evacuation were within the perimeter; but the operation continued until 3 June. Nearly 200,000 British and 139,000 French troops reached England, but the loss of equipment, apart from personal weapons, was total.

VII

BURMA

I WAS visiting our coast defences in the Isle of Wight in the spring of 1942 when I received an urgent message from the Chief of the Imperial General Staff to report to him at once. I left that afternoon and arrived in London in the evening, to be told that I was to proceed at once to take over command of the army in Burma. I said, 'What do you mean by at once?' The answer was, 'At once, within a few hours.'

The Japanese advance from Thailand into Burma had begun on 16 January 1942, and we had suffered a succession of reverses. Within a month Rangoon itself had been threatened.

I went back to my house near Windsor to pack my things and left immediately for Hurn Airport, near Southampton, where an aircraft was waiting to take me and others, including Wingate and a number of R.A.F. officers, to Egypt. As we had to fly across occupied France and the Mediterranean, which was still in enemy hands, the weather had to be right. It was sufficiently wrong to delay our departure, day by day, for a week, so I spent the next seven days motoring from my home to Hurn and back.

Eventually we took off in a Flying Fortress and flew at an altitude of somewhere between twenty and thirty thousand feet—it was frightfully cold and uncomfortable. We were shot at by German anti-aircraft guns over France but escaped the German fighters. After a flight of sixteen or seventeen hours we touched down in Egypt, where I took another plane for India, and then on to Burma. I reached Rangoon on 5 March—too late to save the situation.

In Rangoon, I found that the remnants of 17 Division, which had lost most of its artillery at the crossing of the Sittang River, was holding a defensive position around Pegu, about fifty miles north of Rangoon, and was separated from Burma 1 Division at Toungoo by over 125 miles. Through the heavily wooded country between these two divisions, the Japanese had been infiltrating, with the undoubted object of encircling our left flank and seizing our base at Rangoon behind our backs.

It was clear to me that there was only one possible move to save the situation—which was indeed serious—and that was to prevent any further infiltration by closing the gap between 17 Division and Burma 1 Division and uniting the two formations. I therefore ordered 17 Division to attack northwards and the Burma Division to strike south. These attacks were duly launched but failed to make any appreciable ground. The Japanese were already too strongly in position between the two formations.

It was clear that the retention of Rangoon was impossible with the forces at my disposal, dispersed as they were and with half of them already encircled. The day after my arrival I therefore ordered the evacuation to begin at daylight the following morning, and the demolition of the port and its installations to be carried out thereafter as quickly as possible. I could not save Rangoon but I could save the Army, with luck. The loss of our base would be a most serious matter, as we should have to depend on the scattered stores and dumps spread about in central and northern Burma. When these were used up, the Army would be crippled unless supplies could be sent in over the mountains from India; but, apart from a few mule tracks, communication with India was non-existent. It seemed that we must do the best with what we had. With Chinese assistance—however doubtful—we should be able at least to make the Japanese advance into Burma slow and costly. Such were the thoughts in my mind when I ordered the destruction and evacuation of Rangoon.

As the campaign progressed it became increasingly clear that we were not strong enough to do more than slow down the enemy's advance; and that, eventually, to save the Army, I should have to get it back to India. If I could delay the Japanese until the monsoon broke, time would be gained for the Indian forces to man the frontier and save the eastern states of India from any Japanese incursion.

Work was started at once to improve the virtually non-existent communications from Mandalay to Imphal; and, in the final withdrawal over the Chindwin River, although we had to abandon all our wheeled vehicles, in the third week of May the last soldier of the old Burma Army crossed over the frontier with the monsoon at his heels.

The evacuation of Burma was a complete military defeat—and we had been beaten in a straightforward fight by an enemy who was not greatly superior in numbers but whose troops had been trained in, and equipped for, jungle warfare. Our troops were not.

In our operations we were tied to the only two roads that run north and south from Mandalay to Rangoon, because the Army's transport was composed entirely of wheeled vehicles which could not operate off the roads. Furthermore, the Japanese had complete control of the air, while we had no air support after the loss of Rangoon. What remained of the Burma Army was eventually saved from the wreck of the campaign more by luck than by anything else.

Looking back over the years with the knowledge I now have of the situation that existed when I took over command early in March 1942, I realize that I ought to have ordered an earlier evacuation of Burma. But at the time I was not prepared to admit defeat before I had done everything possible. This delay resulted in the whole of our forces in the south of Burma being encircled and gave the Japanese the chance to destroy them as organized formations—and they missed their chance!

Still, I don't admit that we would have had to lay down our arms in surrender. If we could not have broken through the road block at Pegu which barred our way to the north I was prepared to order units, groups, and individuals to save themselves by fighting their way out, or, by working through the jungle, to join up at Tharrawaddy in the Irrawaddy Valley, where we could re-form. Of course, we would have lost all our transport and heavy equipment, but those who got through would still have had their personal weapons and would have been there to fight another day.

Fortunately for us, the Japanese withdrew the road block, which had probably been a strong flank guard for their encircling forces, and the way was opened for us to the Irrawaddy Valley.

Later in the campaign, when we were joined by the Chinese, I learned that they would fight in defence of an area, even accepting encirclement, and then under cover of darkness slip away through the thick jungle and join up farther north. This delightfully elastic manoeuvre apparently had no adverse effect on their morale. In spite of the fact that they never won a battle against the Japs they were always smiling and jolly and in the best of spirits. Most of them were fine-looking young men of big stature, but they were very poorly equipped, even to the extent of only one rifle to three men: one carried the rifle, the next carried the ammunition for it, and the third carried the food.

Only one Chinese army, the Fifth—and this formation was no stronger than a very weak British division—possessed artillery. These pieces were, I think, either the old French 75 mm. of the First World War, or the German 77 mm. of the same period: yet this army had the reputation of being the best in the whole of the Chinese forces, and I think it was.

Before the battle for Mandalay I went round the front to inspect our defences and was much impressed to see how cleverly this Chinese Fifth Army had dug in its field guns, which were well sited and carefully camouflaged. When contact had been gained with the advancing Japanese I again visited the front, and to my astonishment I found that all the artillery had disappeared.

When I asked the army commander what had happened to his guns he said that he had withdrawn them to safety.

'Then you mean,' I said, 'that they will take no part in the battle?'

'Exactly,' he replied.

'But then what use are they?'

He said: 'General, the Fifth Chinese Army is our best army, because it is the only one which has any field guns, and I cannot afford to risk those guns. If I lose them the Fifth Army will no longer be our best.'

Brave and friendly as they were, the so-called armies of the Chinese were a serious administrative burden. They arrived in Burma with no proper medical organization, and they also expected me to feed them. Since I was desperately short of all types of supplies for my own forces I can only call the Chinese administrative parasites. Furthermore, they were not allowed to undertake any operational role I gave them until it had been agreed to by their Generalissimo, Chiang Kai-shek. Since communications with Chunking were so slow as to be almost non-existent I had virtually no operational control over them.

The American general, Joseph Stilwell, was Chiang Kai-shek's representative with his armies in Burma, and it was through him that I worked. He was quite a character and a tough little man;

his nickname, 'Vinegar Joe', suited him like a glove. He had much to bear from his subordinates. One of them was known for short as General Doo; another as General Di. Unhappily, as was remarked at the time, General Di did, but Doo didn't.

I don't think that Stilwell had much of an opinion of us British, personally he and I got on well together. I always felt that he disliked his position with the Chinese: he was a very senior American general and probably had the feeling that he ought to have been playing a greater part in the war, instead of being relegated to a backwater.

I am aware that most British accounts are unsympathetic to 'Vinegar Joe'—if only for his practice of cussing' the British troops under his command beyond the point of endurance; but—to quote an anonymous commentator—Stilwell knew well (none better after his experience with the American Marauders and with his some-times impossible Chinese) that disaster overtook any army whenever it passed a strange and possibly movable psychological breaking-point where hard-pressed Allied troops suddenly sat down and fell sick, and hard-pressed Japs sat down and actually died.

Certainly, in those dark days he was no defeatist; on the contrary, he showed great courage and fight. When the campaign collapsed he found his way back to India through the jungle on foot, having done all he could for his Chinese forces.

Before we leave the story of this unhappy campaign I must mention two officers who played a major role in saving the Burma Army. Soon after the evacuation of Rangoon, Lieutenant-General Tom Hutton, who worked so ably as my chief of staff, was recalled to India and was replaced by General Jack Winterton. Winterton was invaluable to me and carried the burden which all chiefs of staff have to shoulder with great distinction; a wise, cheerful, and fine staff officer, and a very agreeable companion.

Since my responsibilities as C.-in-C. in Burma were too varied and widespread to be concerned only with the direction of the two British divisions, I formed 17 Division and Burma 1 Division into a corps and asked for General Slim from India to command this new set-up. I could not have asked for a finer man. A great fighting commander, he was to make his name not only in this campaign, but as the victorious commander of the forces that later recaptured Burma from the Japanese, and turned defeat into victory.

BATTLE MAPS

Burma

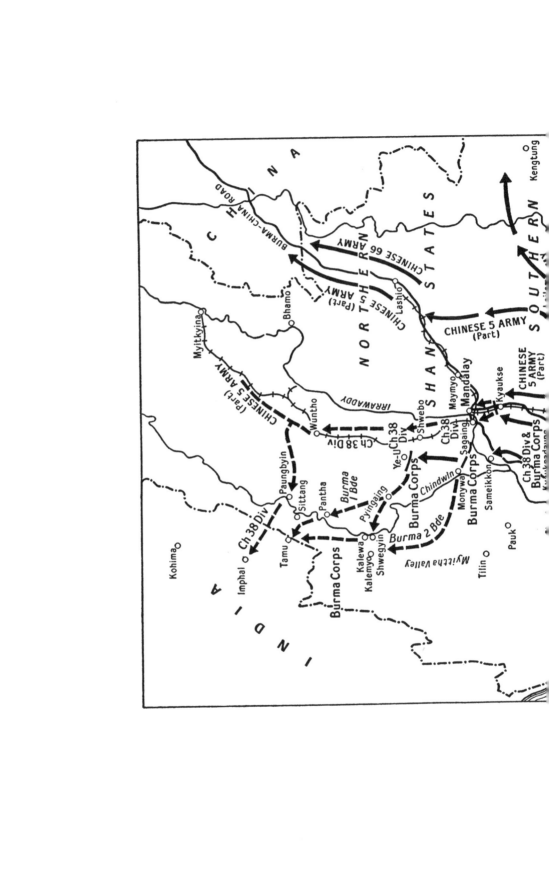

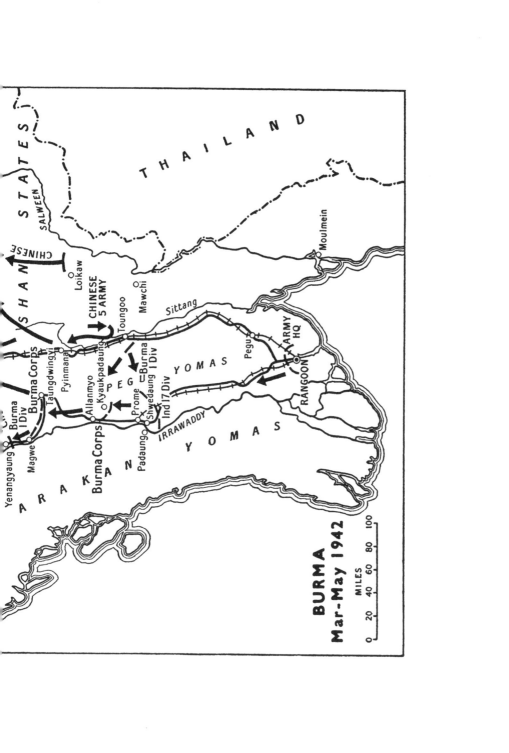

THAILAND

SHAN STATES

SALWEEN

CHINESE

Loikaw

CHINESE 5 ARMY

Toungoo

Mawchi

Moulmein

Sittang

Pyinmana

Burma Corps

Taungdwingyi

Allanmyo

Kyaukpadaung

Burma 1 Div

PEG

YOMAS

Pegu

ARMY HQ

Burma 1 Div

Magwe

Prome

Shwedaung

Ind 17 Div

RANGOON

Burma Corps

Padaung

IRRAWADDY

Yenangyaung

ARAKAN

YOMAS

**BURMA
Mar-May 1942**

MILES

0   20   40   60   80   100

Burma

March–May 1942

WHEN I arrived in Rangoon at the beginning of March 1942, charged with the defence of Burma, the Japanese had already crossed the Lower Sittang, where Indian 17 Division had suffered a near disaster, and were threatening to envelop Rangoon. If the city were to fall, sea communications with India would be severed—and land communications were virtually non-existent. If Burma itself were lost, the land link with China would be lost, and the way would lie open for a Japanese invasion of India.

I left Rangoon just before its fall and flew north to establish Army H.Q. at Maymyo, beyond Mandalay. On 13 March I returned to Prome, where Slim was to organize all available forces to form Burma Corps. I had Burma 1 Division and Indian 17 Division now much under strength and lacking equipment; and the newly arrived 7 Armoured Brigade. No further reinforcement could be expected; and, after 23 March, when the airfield at Magwe was attacked by Japanese bombers, no air force remained for support and reconnaissance. Furthermore, the breakdown of the civil administration and the flood of refugees, hampered military operations.

At this time Indian 17 Division was about thirty miles south of Prome and Burma 1 Division near Toungoo on the other side of the jungle-clad hills called the Pegu Yomas. Relief for Burma 1 Division could be counted on by the arrival of part of Chinese Fifth Army, under Stilwell's command. The plan was for Burma Corps to concentrate for the defence of the Irrawaddy valley, while the Chinese held the front in the valley of the Sittang. To assist this concentration of force, Indian 17 Division was withdrawn northward for the close defence of Prome.

On 24 March the Japanese attacked those columns of Chinese Fifth Army that had reached Toungoo. The town was lost, and the Chinese retreated up the Sittang valley to Pyinmana. To relieve pressure on the Chinese, Indian 17 Division and 7 Armoured Brigade attacked at Shwedaung, with heavy losses on both sides. On 1 April the Japanese attacked Prome in force and, after a fierce struggle, Indian 17 Division, with the armour, effected a fighting withdrawal to Kyaukpadaung–Allanmyo, where Burma 1 division joined the front.

Now the immediate purpose was to protect the oil wells at Yenangyaung and defend Upper Burma; but it was still imperative to maintain contact with the Chinese. I therefore ordered a further withdrawal of Burma Corps in order to stand on the line Magwe— on the Irrawaddy—to Taungdwingyi. I had arranged for the Chinese to extend westward and take over the last-named town; but they failed to put in an appearance.

On 10 April the Japanese struck hard again; and, in spite of some local successes, Burma 1 Division was forced to withdraw from the region of Magwe. The retreat was covered by armour; but the enemy followed up quickly, and the division was soon on the road to the oilfields at Yenangyaung. Bodies of Japanese had already infiltrated into the town before the division's arrival, and the sabotaging of the oilfields was now inevitable. These advanced bodies of Japanese had fought their way through to the Pin Chaung on the northern side, while 38 Division of Chinese Sixth Army—lent to Burma Corps— attacked, with limited success, the Japanese now well established on the south side of the Pin Chaung. Eventually Burma 1 Division fought its way out on foot, and continued northward, covered by the Chinese division and 7 Armoured Brigade.

The position of Indian 17 Division, still retained in and about Taungdwingyi, was now precarious. For disaster had overtaken the Chinese in the Shan States. Mawchi was lost, and by 18 April, the Chinese Sixth Army had been driven north of Loikaw. When the Japanese reached Loilem the remnants of Chinese Sixth Army fled for home up the Burma Road; and although a division of the Chinese Fifth Army from Pyinmana, under Stilwell's personal command, attacked and recaptured Taunggyi, Ho-Pong, and Loilem, very shortly it was to move up the Loilem–Lashio road to join in the general retreat to China. Yet another Chinese Army—rather inscrutably described as the Sixty-Sixth—had been detailed to defend the Lashio area; but the Japanese entered the town on 29 April, and the Chinese Sixty-Sixth Army also took the road for home. Now the only Chinese troops remaining in Burma were the remnants of the Fifth Army who had streamed past Meiktila towards Mandalay, and 38 Division with Burma Corps.

The Japanese were in Bhamo on 4 May and in Myitkyina on 8 May, and it was obvious that Burma Corps must retreat into India without delay. By the 25th it was back on a weak, extended line from Chauk, on the Irrawaddy, to Meikta, Indian 17 Division having now withdrawn from Taungdwingyi. This division, with 7 Armoured Brigade, was soon at Kyaukse, covering the Irrawaddy crossings at Mandalay: farther west the remainder of the corps was retreating towards the river. After a series of rearguard actions Indian 17 Division and 7 Armoured Brigade crossed the Irrawaddy by the Ava bridge, which was then wrecked. Burma 1 Division used ferries at Sameikkon. By 28 April, the whole corps, together with Chinese 38 Division, was beyond the river along a line from Sagaing to Monywa on the Chindwin. The Chinese parted company with the corps at Ye-U, going north to Wuntho and eventually reaching not China but India, by way of Paungybin and the Upper Chindwin.

On 5 May the retreat was resumed, after dumps of supplies had been formed along the track leading to the Chindwin. Burma 1 Brigade was despatched across country to strike the Chindwin at Pantha. On 16 May it arrived at Tamu, on the Indian frontier. Burma 2 Brigade, which had withdrawn up the west bank of the Irrawaddy, also moved independently, following the Myittha valley to rejoin at Kalemyo. The main column reached Shwegyin on the Chindwin, where the troops, still under fierce land and air attack, were embarked on river steamers to be taken upstream for six miles to Kalewa. Tanks and much of the transport had to be destroyed before embarkation. 48 Brigade was taken farther upstream to Sittang, whence they marched through the hills to Tamu. The main body of Burma Corps also arrived at Tamu, after undertaking the ninety-mile march up the Kabaw valley. The Burma rescue operation—as I have to regard it—was over.

Italy

VIII

SICILY IN THIRTY-EIGHT DAYS

A T THE Casablanca Conference, January 1943, I was assigned to the operational command of 'Husky'—the code-name for the invasion of Sicily. The planning of it was not to be easy: hardly surprisingly, in view of the fact that the planners were distributed over at least four centres—Cairo, Algiers, Malta, and the United Kingdom. I am aware, too, of the feeling that had General Patton—as was the original intention—been allowed to land in the north-west of the island he would have got to Messina by sheer drive of personality, and blocked the German escape route across the Straits. For reasons that will appear in this narrative I cannot agree. I would remind the reader that Sicily, so far from being a placid terrain, is highly mountainous; and it remains my conviction that the Allied troops engaged in the operation showed reasonable expedition.

Sicily was the first large-scale amphibious operation against enemy-held beaches in the Second World War. It was, therefore, without any practical experience that the planners began their task. Apart from the many assault problems to be solved, such as beach gradients, tides, hostile defensive positions, strength and location of German and Italian forces, it was obviously essential for us to have a port or ports through which to supply the troops fighting inland.

There were four good ports with the necessary capacity; Messina, Catania, Syracuse and Palermo. Messina was heavily guarded by fixed defences and beyond the range of our fighters. Catania was only just within fighter cover, and was also heavily defended and under the fighter umbrella of the Luftwaffe based on the Catania group of airfields, within close striking distance of the port. Syracuse and Palermo were both within our fighter cover and not so heavily defended.

The soundest administrative plan was to base the British Eighth

Army on Syracuse and the United States Seventh Army on Palermo; but there was a strategic weakness in that the two Allied armies would not initially be within supporting distance of each other, and thereby exposed to the risk of being held in detail.

The estimate of enemy strength at the time was two German divisions, six Italian mobile divisions, and five Italian coastal divisions. Against this garrison we were bringing a force of just over ten divisions, with two more in reserve.

Thus from the point of view of numbers we enjoyed no actual superiority, although we had the initiative to attack when and where we chose, together with command of the sea and a somewhat doubtful degree of superiority in the air over the coming battle fields. Moreover, it must be borne in mind that this estimate of the relative strength of the opposing forces took no count of the fact that there was nothing to prevent the Axis from reinforcing their garrison in Sicily once they surmised that an invasion was imminent.

There was another factor: Air Chief Marshal Tedder pointed out that the Comiso–Gela airfield centre, inland from the south coast, had been developed into a first-class air base, and that, unless it could be captured for our own use, our air force would labour under an intolerable handicap. Admiral Cunningham also stated that the risk of allowing enemy air forces to operate from this south-eastern group of airfields would be unacceptable to the naval arm.

For these various reasons, and in view of the strong representations made by the Eighth Army that the Allied forces should be within supporting distance, the original plan, under which the Americans were to land at the north-west corner of the island, was recast. The arguments for strengthening the east coast assault and for the early capture of the airfields were overwhelmingly strong.

During this period of planning I myself was actively engaged in the field, conducting the final phase of the battle for Tunis, and was thus unable to give my whole attention to the ideas of the planning staff working in Algiers. The position in which I found myself illustrates the difficulties with which a commander-in-chief can be faced when involved in two entirely different situations simultaneously.

In dealing with Sicily I had to take an administrative risk or a tactical risk. I inclined to the tactical risk—that is, I gave priority

The King and Queen at an artillery demonstration in southern England in 1940, during their tour of the defences under Southern Command. Note the Queen shielding her ears against the roar of the guns.

With Churchill and General Montgomery on one of the Prime Minister's visits to North Africa, August 1942. Winston liked to wear his 'siren suit' on such occasions. Alex later recalled, 'In Italy, Winston was always bothering me to take him up to the front to see a battle.'

Field Marshal Erwin Rommel. Through the Ultra *decrypts, Alex recognised one or two Afrika Korps officers. They had served together in the Baltic* Landwehr *against the Bolsheviks in 1920.*

Alex with Field Marshal Smuts, Prime Minister of South Africa, and Sir Miles Lampson (later Lord Killearn), British Ambassador to Egypt, in Cairo, October 1942.

With General Dick McCreery, an expert on armoured fighting vehicles.

General Bernard Freyberg VC and General Brian Horrocks

An infantry platoon at Alamein with fixed bayonets advancing through shell-bursts. Note the shadow of one falling across the line of soldiers.

The guns of Alamein, 23 October 1942

Bruce Scott, Wise, Alexander, Wavell, Slim and 'Taffy' Davies in Burma, 1942.

Dunkirk harbour, June 1940

Prime Minister's conference in Algiers, June 1943: From left, Anthony Eden, Alan Brooke, Tedder, Cunningham, Alexander, Marshall, Eisenhower and Montgomery.

With General Eisenhower waiting for a military parade to form up. Alex and 'Ike' forged a strong relationship during the campaign and became firm friends for the rest of their lives, rekindling their friendship when Alex later became Governor-General of Canada.

A Valentine Mk2 light infantry tank entering Tripoli in January 1943 carrying, among others, a regimental piper. Note that the unit's identity has been obscured by the censor. (Photograph from an unknown publication.)

Alex and Montgomery in Italy, November 1943. (By permission of The Imperial War Museum/ TA_004562)

General 'Vinegar Joe' Stilwell, an acerbic and ruthless commander.

With General Omar Bradley, a competent American commander who, unlike Patton, got on very well with the British. It made Alex's job considerably easier. Alex seldom wore a beret, preferring the peaked cap with its scarlet band. He always wore this at the front despite its obvious attraction to enemy snipers. He never ever put on a steel helmet.

Coming ashore at Salerno with Mark Clark and Dick McCreery. Note heavy equipment landing craft in the background.

Taking the salute at a joint services parade in Tunis with Mark Clark and General Juin of the French army. Juin is saluting with his left hand as he sustained serious injuries to his right arm in the First World War.

With General John Harding, his loyal chief of staff. Short in stature, long in achievements.

Conducting a conference on the bonnet of his staff car. Generals Montgomery, Richardson, Alex, Bedell Smith and Patton in Sicily. Alex was often obliged to mediate between Monty and Patton who always had an uneasy relationship under his command.

Driving his friend Harold Macmillan, the resident minister and his political adviser, around the ruins of the town of Cassino. The fall of the monastery was on Alex's orders. "No bricks and mortar, however sacrosanct, should take precedence over men's lives." (The Union Jack is tied to a pole on the roadside and is not attached to the jeep!)

With His Majesty King George VI on one of his visits to the battlegrounds in the Liri Valley. The King was given the use of a caravan during his stay. He complained during dinner one evening that his bath 'al fresco' had olive leaves floating in the water.

With General Anders, an enterprising cavalry officer in the Tsar's army in the First World War. He commanded a Polish corps under Alex and was later prominent in Poland's post-war government-in-exile in London.

With Marshal Josef Tito studying a map on the terrace of the White Palace, Belgrade, 24 February 1945. It was Tito's official residence and previously occupied by King Peter II, who was deposed in 1941. (By permission of The Imperial War Museum/ NA_022637)

A gaslit 'summit' conference at the Foreign Office, Athens, 27 December 1944. Harold Macmillan on Alex's left; Greece's representative, the formidable Archbishop Damaskinos (in the chair), Winston Churchill and Anthony Eden on his right.

Final surrender in Italy, 12 noon, 2 May 1945. Two German officials – in civilian clothes – representing General von Vietinghoff and Obergruppenführer Wolff, and the Allied representatives, led by Lieutenant-General Morgan, Alex's chief of staff.

With Marshal Tolbukhin of the Red Army, centre, and Colonel-General Jeltof (the political commissar and effectively senior to the marshal) in February/ March 1945. Alex is wearing on his right breast the Star of Yugoslavia having just been awarded it by Tito.

Alex's mobile HQ at Lake Bolsena. Two army lorries converted into sleeping and working quarters. In this photo there appears to be precious little shade or cover. Not so important perhaps when the Allies enjoyed air superiority.

Addressing his troops, who appear to be in high spirits. His ADC Rupert Clarke is on the far right.

Buckingham Palace with HM the King celebrating the Irish Guards' Golden Jubilee in June 1950. Alex had flown over from Canada where he was serving as Governor-General.

Right: *With the Queen and the Earl of Home at the Bowes Lyon family home in Hertfordshire. The Queen was born Lady Elizabeth Bowes Lyon and had spent her early childhood there.* C. 1950s.

Below: *Inspecting a Guard of Honour of German troops* Wehrbereichskommando *during British Week in Düsseldorf, Germany, 25 May 1964. Note roundel on cap of German escorting officer, similar to those worn on its army's uniform since before the First World War.*

to the airfields—for two reasons. First, there was a reasonable prospect in July of good weather for beach maintenance; and secondly, the advent of the DUKW—an ingenious amphibious vehicle, unfamiliar to us at the time—persuaded me that it would solve our difficulties of maintaining a large force over open beaches.

After seeing this new vehicle in operation I made the decision to put the United States Seventh Army ashore on the open beaches on the left of the Eighth Army, which would land just south of Syracuse. Certainly the decision represented a risk, but it was a calculated risk.

Such, then, was the final plan to which I agreed. Under it the two Allied armies would land and fight shoulder to shoulder to reduce the island.

In the invasion of Sicily we used airborne troops in the assault for the first time. From my temporary advanced headquarters in Malta I went to Delemara, on the coast, after dark to watch the gliders fly past for the landings in support of the invasion forces. It was blowing hard and the roar of the aircraft towing the gliders was partly carried away.

Because of the high wind, many of the gliders were scattered over a wide area on landing and missed their objectives; others came down in the sea off the coast and were lost. However, despite dispersion, these airborne landings behind the defences in the south-eastern corner of the island were of sterling assistance to the assaulting troops.

The swell raised by the gale caused some delay in the assault landings themselves. On the other hand, at many points along the coast the garrisons had relaxed their vigil, vainly imagining that no landings would be attempted in such weather. We thus achieved a measure of surprise beyond our expectations.

I must emphasize that in order to obtain concentration of force I was proceeding on sound strategic lines but at the expense of administrative doctrine and experience. Furthermore, I was not unmindful of the fact that the plan might well appear to give the American troops the heavier task, as they could not have the use of a port until they had taken Palermo, on the other side of the island.

I therefore quote from my despatch: 'I wish to place on record here that General Patton at once fell in with my new plan, the military advantages of which were as clear to him as to me: and neither he nor anyone in Seventh Army raised any form of objection. It is an impressive example of the spirit of complete loyalty and inter-Allied co-operation which inspired all operations with which I was associated in the Mediterranean theatre.'

Once firmly ashore the two Allied armies set about securing the island, an operation that went according to plan. The Eighth Army were veterans, except for the Canadian 1 Division, who had their first battle experience of the war; and under their fine and able commander, General Guy Simmonds, they soon showed their qualities as fighting men, a reputation to which they greatly added during the Italian campaign.

Most of the American formations were also new to battle, but they, too, showed dash and initiative under General George Patton. In the result this heavily garrisoned and strongly fortified island was overrun in thirty-eight days. The first landings were in the early hours of 10 July 1943; on the night of 16 August the leading troops of the United States 3 Division entered Messina, to be joined next morning by commando elements of the Eighth Army.

The capture of Sicily gave us an important strategic advantage. It opened up the Mediterranean theatre and gave us a firm base from which to conduct further operations against southern Europe. Indeed, it heralded the surrender of Italy within little more than a fortnight. We were about to implement in full measure the directive given to General Eisenhower, as Commander-in-Chief, Allied Force, after the 'Trident' Conference in Washington of May 1943, to carry out such operations in exploitation of the conquest of Sicily as would be best calculated to contain the maximum number of German divisions: a directive that I inherited, and one that remained in force to the end of the campaign in Italy.

IX

RETURN TO CASERTA

THE Royal Palace at Caserta, twenty-one miles north-east of Naples, looks today exactly as I remember it in the days when it was H.Q., Supreme Allied Command, Mediterranean.

One of the biggest, if not the biggest, of all the palaces in Europe, it was built at about the same time as Versailles. I found when I visited it recently that its gardens are well kept and its lawns and flower-beds well cared for. The 'pond'—as we called it—from which General Mark Clark used to take off in his light aircraft when he went to visit the front, had lost its quotation marks and was now indeed a pond. The fountains and the waterfalls, which were out of action in my day, were in full flow, and the park was crowded with happy Italians enjoying the pleasures of the palace gardens.

It was at Caserta that I came up against an unexpected problem amongst my staff, which was half British and half American. They came to me one day and said, 'We are in a great difficulty to which we can find no answer. The Americans, when they arrive at the office, like all the windows tightly shut and the British like all the windows open. Can you help us to find a solution?'

I suggested that whoever arrived first at the office could have the windows as he liked for the day—British or American: a solution that worked extremely well. Thereafter my staff not only arrived on time, but, more often than not, ahead of time!

Caserta is also associated in my mind, and very pleasantly, with Harold Macmillan. I had known him from the days of the First World War, when he was an officer in the Grenadiers, but it was not until he came to Italy as Resident Minister and Winston Churchill's political representative that I got to know him as an intimate friend. The role of Resident Minister was a political appointment

—he was the Prime Minister's personal representative within a defined theatre of operations. As such he acted as adviser to the commander-in-chief on all political issues, thereby leaving him free to devote his main energies to the problems of the battlefield. Thus in my own command in the Mediterranean I was never brought into direct collision with an Allied government on a political issue. When, for example, political trouble broke out in Greece it was Mr. Macmillan who handled the political side.

For a time in Italy Mr. Macmillan shared my mess at Caserta, and during this period he and I would go to the front in my open desert car to visit the troops. Those were happy days for me. I had a delightful companion who was both wise in advice and always amusing; a man of great intellect, morally and physically brave, but far too reserved to show these admirable qualities outwardly. A Prime Minister cannot hide behind an aloof exterior; and today the country is fortunate to see him as he is—a very fine character and one of the great political figures of our time.

Winston Churchill had warned the Italian people that if they played in with the Germans the Allies would drag 'the red-hot rake of war' through the length and breadth of their lovely land. The warning went unheeded; the threat was fulfilled. But before we move into the sombre months of the war in Italy that lie ahead, I should like to recall one memorable encounter.

Shortly after our troops reached the Arno I remembered that my old friend Osbert Sitwell, whom I had known since the days when he, too, was a subaltern in the Grenadiers before the First World War, owned a villa somewhere in the neighbourhood of Florence, and I found that it was about six miles south of the city. I arranged to visit it.

Montegufoni is much finer and larger than our term 'villa' implies. It is, in fact, what we would perhaps call a manor house—locally it is known as the Castello—with a large, central courtyard. It stands on a hill surrounded by vineyards from which an excellent wine is produced. During the German occupation it was requisitioned as a minor military headquarters.

It delighted me to learn something of rather more historical interest, namely, that Montegufoni, Germans or no Germans, had housed the most valuable of the pictures from the Uffizi Gallery in Florence. The Italians had built a false wall on one side of the courtyard, and behind it they had secreted such treasures as Botticelli's 'Primavera' and 'The Birth of Venus'.

When I arrived the pictures had been taken from this hiding place and were proudly displayed in the great hall. It was a great moment—thus to be confronted by these great pictures across the havoc of war.

'The red-hot rake of war'—indeed, yes! But there's one comment in this context that I would like to make. Although I cannot pretend that the partisans, despite their personal gallantry, were ever a serious problem to the Germans, they played their part in the Allied cause. In particular, I should like to put on record my appreciation of the help given to our escaping prisoners of war by the good and simple people of Italy. Although their government had surrendered, they were still under enemy domination; and were able to render assistance only at great risk to themselves.

The Italians have brilliantly rebuilt their country: only occasionally does one come across an unmistakable relic of the old battlefields. Nor need one feel surprise. Italy has seen much history; in fact, it is history; and few countries have known such a succession of armed invaders through the centuries. I like the story of the visitor who mentioned 'the war' to a friendly Italian whom he had engaged in conversation. 'Did you speak of the war, Signor? Which war do you mean? There have been so many—it is so confusing.'

On 3 September 1943, in a tent in an almond grove near Cassibile, in Sicily, General Walter Bedell Smith, chief of staff at Allied Force Headquarters, on behalf of and in the presence of General Eisenhower, and General Castellano, a member of the Italian Commando Supremo, on behalf of Marshal Badolgio, head of the Italian Government after the fall of Mussolini on 25 July, signed the Military Terms of the Italian Surrender. Thirteen hours before, to the thunder of six hundred guns in the Straits of Messina, the Eighth Army had begun the first invasion of the continent of Europe.

At a quarter to eight on the evening of 8 September, when the invasion force was already heading up the Gulf of Salerno, the Marshal came on the air to announce the Italian surrender and to inform the Italian people that they were now pledged to fight on the side of the Allies. The assaulting troops were at once seized with a definite feeling of optimism; the Germans were shocked into action. During the nine hours that remained to them they took over the Italian coast defence positions and disarmed the Italian garrisons. When the first Allied troops landed the Germans were in readiness. So opened the campaign in Italy.

X

THE WAR IN ITALY

SALERNO

LUCK may play a great part in war, but I prefer an efficient Guardian Angel such as attended me, despite deep disappointments and serious setbacks, in the operations at Salerno, Cassino and Anzio.

The object of the Salerno landings, on 9 September 1943, was to enable us to seize a port as far north in Italy as possible, from which firm base we could maintain strong forces on the mainland.

Naples was the port chosen. But because it was too strongly defended to be carried by assault from the sea, suitable landing beaches as near to Naples as possible were studied, and those of Salerno proved the best, for three reasons:

1. They were within easy striking distance of Naples;
2. They were within fighter cover of our air forces based in Sicily—but only just; and
3. They offered a continuous stretch of beach about twenty miles long, with excellent underwater gradients.

The size of our land forces was restricted to what the Navy could carry, and this proved to be two corps. Generally speaking, when I was planning operations with our allies I rightly or wrongly—I think rightly—tried as far as possible to let the Americans share the hazards as well as the fruits of victory with the British. So, for the Salerno operation, which was known as 'Avalanche', British X Corps and United States VI Corps were selected; and the force was under the command of General Mark Clark, C.-in-C. of the United States Fifth Army. The British Eighth Army under

Montgomery was already operating in the toe of Italy, where it had landed on 3 September.

For an amphibious operation the Salerno beaches were excellent; but there were unpleasant obstacles to be overcome before the port of Naples could be reached. The coast is hemmed in by mountains, and it was necessary for a pass through one of these to be seized by our forces.

Some may think that we should have landed farther north, in the coastal plain of the Volturno, from which an easy run for armour could have been undertaken direct to Naples. The actual landing beaches were not nearly so good as those of the Bay of Salerno, but such an operation, if successful, would have given us the strategic advantage of landing in the rear of all the German forces operating from Naples to the south.

It is interesting to reflect that this is where Field-Marshal Kesselring, the German Commander-in-Chief South, thought we might land, and in consequence reinforced this part of the coast with two divisions. He is on record to have stated that Salerno was 'indeed a uniquely suitable place to land'; but the statement is to be found in his memoirs, written some six or seven years after the event. Anyway, he chose to ignore the German Supreme Command directive of 18 August, which read: 'In the coastal area, from Naples to Salerno, which primarily is the most threatened, a strong group of at least three mobile formations is to be assembled. All elements of the army that are no longer mobile are to be moved to this area.' I remain satisfied with our choice. The factor which weighed most strongly in my mind was that the landing must be under fighter cover; and it still seems strange to me that the Germans, who are such good soldiers, should apparently have ignored the necessity for air superiority in an amphibious operation of this sort—or perhaps they were inexcusably ignorant of the limited range of our fighters.

As it turned out, our landing at Salerno saw some extremely anxious days before we were firmly established ashore, although we were opposed only by the Hermann Göring and 16 Panzer Division and some other German elements.

My conclusion is that if the Navy and the Army had not enjoyed air superiority at Salerno the operation would have failed. I myself was in the beachhead during the fighting, and am in a position to pay tribute to the guns of *Warspite* and *Valiant* in halting the German counter-offensive. Nor do I overlook the equally valuable contribution made by the heavy bombing attacks of the Strategic Air Force.

A few months ago I revisited the area, now a battleground for the holiday-maker. On the way from Positano to Salerno we stopped at Maiori, a little town and port. It was here that the American Rangers landed at night and scaled the heights overlooking the main road from Vietri to Naples.

When one sees the ground again and studies the precipitous terrain they had to climb, one realizes what a great feat of arms was performed that night. When they reached the heights they still had quite a hard fight to gain control of the mountains overlooking the pass. It is obvious that the American Rangers' manoeuvre was a key contribution in our advances from the plains of Salerno across the mountain pass into the Naples plain.

Some ten miles south-east of Salerno and five miles inland lies Battaglia which, together with its airfield, was one of the British objectives in the landing. However, X Corps, under Dick McCreery, couldn't quite make it and was held just short of the place, which wasn't taken until eight or nine days after the initial landings, when the town was pretty well wiped out by the Strategic Air Force.

Incidentally, it was not until I arrived back at the beachhead from visiting this particular section of the front, five or six days after the landings, with 'Ginger' Hawkesworth, commanding the 46 Division, and Mark Clark, to discuss the situation and observe the German positions, that I learned of the latter's quite impossible suggestion to transfer the American beachhead to the British sector. Happily, by that evening—15 September—the crisis was over.

But with Battaglia in our hands we were still faced by a quite high feature just to the north, which the Germans held and which we were not able to take until they started pulling out. It was of high importance because it gave the Germans all the advantage of observation throughout the whole of these operations.

The river Sele separated the United States Corps and the British Corps, and down it the Germans made their great counter-attack, when they got to within about half a mile of the coast. If they had pushed on to the sea their arrival might have caused us some embarrassment, but I don't think it would have been disastrous, unless they had found themselves able to fan out and attack both right and left, and thus clean up our beaches.

At the same time, they would have found themselves in a dangerous pocket; and if we could have pinched out their counter-attack the whole effort might have turned out to our advantage. However, they were not strong enough to get to the coast, and we held their attack, pushed them back, and got the objectives we had set for our break-out.

Throughout the battle the Eighth Army were advancing rapidly from the toe of Italy and working their way round the rear of the German defences. I think it was this threat, more than anything else, that caused the Germans to pull out, and so gave us the opportunity of using our armoured division, which we had kept in reserve to thrust through the gap in the mountains from Vietri into the plain of Naples.

The Germans in their counter-attacks had been working under definite limitations of time. They had, deliberately, as good as broken contact with Eighth Army in order to fling the troops coming up from Calabria against Fifth Army; but they could not ignore Eighth Army's advance beyond a certain date. By the 15th they decided that they had failed—the day that patrols from Eighth Army made contact with patrols from VI Corps five miles west of Vallo. The enemy had already begun to withdraw in front of VI Corps, and with that confession of his inability to destroy our bridgehead our hold on the mainland of Italy could be considered firm.

Once we traversed the pass beyond Vietri—X Corps was through on 28 September 1943—the Germans had to pull out of Naples, and although their rearguards gave us considerable trouble and delayed our advance, especially between Vesuvius and the sea, they had no natural defensive positions to hold on to until they got back to the Volturno river, which is west of Caserta.

On 3 October, two days after the King's Dragoon Guards had entered Naples, I was able to inform the Prime Minister that I was satisfied with the military prospect. I believed that my armies could pursue their 'stated ends' and, in accordance with a plan already in outline, would be able forthwith to undertake an advance that would carry them north of Rome. The 'stated ends', as I have already noted, laid down at the 'Trident' Conference in

Washington in May 1943, were to carry out such operations in exploitation of the conquest of Sicily as would be best calculated to contain the maximum number of German divisions.

During the next three days, information about German reinforcements reached me that extinguished any false optimism about the prospect ahead. I had to report to General Eisenhower, then Commander-in-Chief, Allied Forces, that the Germans had resolved not to withdraw but to 'stay in Rome and defend it to the utmost of their power'. I warned that further progress would be slow and that direct assault on the enemy's positions in the mountains, now strongly held, must be costly.

Here was the true moment of birth of the Italian campaign. I and my commanders were determined to have Rome, and were not to be deterred by the German resolve to hold it; but Rome was not the end of the story. This side of Rome, and beyond it, the Allied armies were to be faced with a seemingly unending succession of difficulties of terrain—as Winston Churchill remarked, there was 'always something else'; they were to be called upon to fight with resources always inadequate to their tasks; and they were to experience a 'savage versatility' of climate without any parallel in north-west Europe. The axis of any advance northward invariably lay across natural obstacles of rivers or mountains; and, because German demolitions were so efficient and effective, a small rearguard could always put up a fierce battle while the main body went back at its leisure.

The line the Germans decided to hold, known as the 'Winter Line'—a misnomer, since it was not a line but a series of defended positions in depth—had been reconnoitred by them before the Italian surrender. It was based on the east coast on the River Sangro and in the west on the Garigliano, with the strong Cassino position rising to the *massif* of Monte Cairo. The centre of the peninsula, the rugged mountains of the Abruzzi, where bears roamed in the fastnesses of the National Park, was considered too difficult to admit of manoeuvre by large forces. On this line the Italian peninsula is at its narrowest—only eighty-five miles from sea to sea. Delaying positions could be held in front of it in order to gain time for the weather to deteriorate still further and to allow artificial defences to be constructed to add to the natural strength of the whole position.

On 8 November I received a new directive from General Eisenhower. It reaffirmed the objectives given on 25 September—the capture of Rome and the maintenance, subsequently, of maximum pressure on the enemy. The directive recognized that the enemy 'intends to resist our occupation of southern Italy to a greater degree than hitherto contemplated'. But the Fifth Army was already suffering from severe exhaustion; and on 13 November General Clark represented to me that the time had come to pause and regroup. The winter rains had started at the end of September and were steadily increasing, making road and passes extremely difficult and turning the open country into a sea of mud. Eighth Army, at the other end of the Line, in the battle of the Sangro, had driven the enemy from strong prepared positions and inflicted heavy casualties. But thanks to the difficult nature of the ground and the violence of the winter weather, and the enemy's ability to relieve tired troops with fresh, no vital ground had been seized. By the end of December one could only say that the German 'Winter-stellung' had been broken into—but not broken. It was time to seek some other way of opening up the road to Rome.

The Führer Order to stand south of Rome proved of positive assistance in carrying out the Combined Chiefs of Staff directive. If the Germans had adhered to their original intention, it would have been very difficult to carry out my mission of containing the maximum enemy forces: an orderly withdrawal up the peninsula would have required only a comparatively small force, aided by the difficulties of the terrain. Although we had the initiative in operations, the Germans had the initiative in deciding whether we should achieve our object: they were free to refuse to allow themselves to be contained in Italy.

All danger of such an alarming result was removed by Hitler's decision. From the moment of that decision the German Army undertook a commitment as damaging and debilitating as Napoleon's Peninsular campaign, the final result of which was that it saw itself next summer under the deplorable necessity of pouring troops into Italy to retrieve disaster at the very moment when the Allied invading forces were storming the breaches of the crumbling West Wall.

CASSINO

The route to Rome leads naturally through the Liri Valley; and the enemy's main defensive front, covering the Liri Valley, which is flanked on either side by mountains, was one of the strongest natural positions in Italy. Here the German plan of defence rested on three fortified positions known as the 'Gustav', 'Adolf Hitler', and 'Caesar' lines. The first of these was the present main line of resistance. It represented the rear line of the old 'Winterstellung', which had withstood many furious attacks. Nevertheless, as early as December 1943, work had started on the 'Adolf Hitler'.

At the gateway to this route stands Monte Cassino, dominating the whole position; and on the summit of Monte Cassino stands the large, massively built monastery with its perfect observation and sheltering walls.

The battle for Cassino—or rather the series of battles for Cassino—began on 17 January 1944, when X Corps attacked across the Garigliano. On 20 January, United States II Corps attacked across the Rapido, but this blow failed and X Corps, after meeting with some initial success, were checked by heavy counter-attacks. One more attack began on 16 February, and it was this assault that was preceded by the destruction of the monastery by bombing and artillery fire. But Cassino town and the monastery were not to be captured until 18 May, when the Poles raised the red and white standard with the white eagle over the ruins of the monastery.

Till the February bombardment, the great Benedictine monastery had been spared deliberately, to our detriment. Whether the Germans took advantage of its deep cellars for shelter and its high windows for observation I do not know; but it was obvious that this huge and massive building offered the defenders considerable protection from hostile fire, merely by their sheltering under its walls. As Winston Churchill has observed, the enemy fortifications were hardly separate from the building itself.

There now occurred a curious and slightly comical incident. An American officer on the Intelligence Staff reported that an enemy conversation picked up on the wireless seemed to offer conclusive proof that the Germans were inside the monastery. The intercepted conversation ran: 'Wo ist der Abt? Ist er noch im Kloster?' (Where is the 'Abt'? Is it still in the monastery?)

'Abt' is the German military abbreviation for 'abteilung',

meaning a section. But unfortunately 'Abt' also means 'Abbot', and since 'Abt' is masculine and 'abteilung' femine, the conversation referred to the Abbot—if it had referred to the section it would have been, 'Wo ist *die* Abt? Ist sie noch im Kloster?' Which goes to show that a little knowledge of a foreign tongue can be a dangerous thing.

It must be appreciated that the Anzio landing, which began on 22 January 1944, had been designed as a pincer movement, to force Kesselring to draw off his strength from the Cassino front to protect his threatened rear, thereby weakening his main front and giving us a good opportunity to break through his winter line.

When it became known to us that a great enemy counter-attack against the Anzio bridgehead was being prepared, and time was therefore of the essence, my chief American air force officer, General John Cannon, said: 'If you let me use the whole of our bomber force against Cassino, we will whip it out like a dead tooth.'

Well, orthodox military methods had failed to break the front—it was time to try something new. But though, on 14 February, over eleven hundred tons of bombs were dropped the move failed, and for two reasons.

First, the attack on the monastery and town did not succeed in breaking the morale of the German soldiers, who fought like demons to hold on to their positions, no matter if those positions had been reduced to a rubble heap—the main defenders were a German parachute division.

Secondly, buildings, when destroyed, can be more valuable to the defenders than intact buildings, as we found now in the town of Cassino below the monastery: badly churned-up ground and piled-up rubble create quite a problem for tanks and infantry. One recalls the Western Front in the First World War, when most major offensives were seriously handicapped by prolonged artillery action turning the battlefield into a quagmire.

After this failure to break the Cassino front I visited our base hospital at Caserta to see our wounded. At the hospital I asked if there were any German wounded, and the answer was that about twenty seriously wounded German soldiers from the 1 Parachute Division were being looked after in a separate ward. So I asked to see them.

When I appeared at the door of their ward the German Feld-webel (sergeant-major), who was very seriously wounded, called his men to attention: 'Achtung, Herr General'—and the wounded men all lay to attention in their beds with their arms outstretched stiffly over the sheets. I had to say: 'Machen Sie weiter' ('Carry on'), or they would have kept their position until further orders.

I mention this incident to illustrate the type of soldiers we were fighting. Whatever we may feel about the Germans, we must admit that German soldiers were extremely tough and brave.

Was the destruction of the monastery a military necessity? Was it morally wrong to destroy it?

The answer to the first question is 'yes'. It was necessary more for the effect it would have on the morale of the attackers than for purely material reasons.

The answer to the second question is this: when soldiers are fighting for a just cause and are prepared to suffer death and muti-lation in the process, bricks and mortar, no matter how venerable, cannot be allowed to weigh against human lives. Every good com-mander must consider the morale and feelings of his fighting men; and, what is equally important, the fighting men must know that their whole existence is in the hands of a man in whom they have complete confidence. Thus the commanding general must make it absolutely clear to his troops that they go into action under the most favourable conditions he has the power to order.

In the context of the Cassino battle, how could a structure which dominated the fighting field be allowed to stand? The monastery had to be destroyed. Withal, everything was done to save the lives of the monks and their treasures: ample warning was given of the bombing.

I reflected again on all these matters when I saw the battlefield recently. Once more, after the passage of years, I realized how tre-mendously rugged and mountainous is the terrain over which we had to fight. Monte Cassino is one of the strongest natural defen-sive positions in the whole of Europe, and it hardly seems credible that we ultimately overcame it.

I saw again Monte Trocchio, which at the time John Harding, then my chief of staff, and I climbed to get a front-line view of Monte Cassino and the Liri Valley; it was not a particularly enjoyable excursion, as the Germans were shelling it, and we had to wait between bursts of gunfire to sprint across open ground to regain cover before making our way finally to the top. There were also uncharted mines, left behind by the Germans when the Americans took the mountain. It was on the slopes of Monte Trocchio that the New Zealand brigade commander, General Kippenberger, lost both of his feet on a land mine when viewing the battlefield shortly after its capture.

At the foot of Monte Trocchio, beside the main road, there is a stone column which marks the beginning of the track which the late King George VI used when he went to visit the battlefields of the Liri Valley on 25 July 1944. By then the engineers had cleared all land mines from the ground over which the King was to pass.

The visitor to Cassino today can hardly imagine what conditions were like during the battle. The place is now at least twice its former size, and modern houses and buildings have replaced the little stone dwellings of the old town. Here and there remain ruins that suggest Roman Tunis rather than houses lived in only seventeen years ago, when Cassino was a sleepy little place in the heart of Italy without experience of war for hundreds of years.

The great Benedictine monastery, from which a magnificent view of the surrounding country can be gained, has been completely rebuilt in cut stone. Both outside and in, it has been restored to its former condition, even down to the marble work and interior decoration.

The bombs of the Allied air forces had left nothing of the building standing except part of one of the outer walls—all else was a heap of rubble. Yet amidst this appalling destruction St. Benedict's tomb, in the centre of the monastery, went utterly unscathed. After the capture and liberation of Rome I was able to tell the late Pope of its survival. He was deeply moved. He assured me, moreover, that he well understood the military necessity for the bombing and the inevitable destruction of the monastery.

I well remember that, when the Allies were in occupation of Rome, crowds of our soldiers went to the Vatican to see the Pope, who daily gave them his blessing. Thinking that it might be too great a strain on him I said one day: 'I hope that all these Allied soldiers are not too great a burden for your Holiness,' and added, 'although of course, so many of them are Catholics.' He replied: 'No! No! Let them all come to me—I love them all.'

In the Cassino war cemetery lie so many of our soldiers who fought in this great battle. The first headstones to be seen mark the graves of the dead of that gallant Canadian Corps who in the final phase took the key position in the Liri Valley at Pontecorvo. It was a strongpoint in the Hitler Line; and here the Canadians found a hole in the German defences which, without further orders, they exploited with great dash and gallantry.

On top of Monte Cassino, just below the monastery, is the Polish cemetery laid out in tiers like a great stone staircase against the rocky mountainside. This imposing memorial marks the final resting-place of those gallant soldiers of the Polish II Corps who fought on the right flank of the Eighth Army and who, in hard and bitter fighting, encircled the monastery to join up with 78 Division.

Seen on a map or viewed from the commanding position of Monastery Hill, the Liri Valley appears to be quite flat. Actually, one finds that it is heavily covered with trees and olive groves, that it is undulating and has quite deep gorges, mostly passable for tanks but far from ideal, as they were continually running blind into anti-tank guns.

Once we were through the Liri Valley we again entered the mountains; and here it was that the French Corps, under Marshal Juin, made such a spectacular advance, assisted by the Goums. These fine mountain warriors from Morocco and southern Algeria climbed and advanced over rocky heights which the Germans thought impassable.

One incident during my visit to these old battlefields amused me. When we were having luncheon at the Excelsior Hotel in Cassino, about twenty smartly dressed Italian officers entered the dining-room. One of our party said jokingly that they were probably a Staff College syndicate come to study the Cassino operations of 1944. We learned that this was exactly who they were and what they were doing!

They would certainly have been interested if they had known that the C.-in-C. of the invading army, his chief of staff (John Harding), and one of his corps commanders (Dick McCreery) during the Cassino battle were in the same room.

ANZIO

Anzio played a vital role in the capture of Rome by giving me the means to employ a double-handed punch—from the beachhead and from Cassino—which caught the Germans in a pincer movement. Without this double-handed punch I do not believe we should ever have been able to break through the German defences at Cassino.

Orders for the operation were issued on 2 January. The objective was defined as to cut the enemy communications and threaten the German rear. Fifth Army was ordered to make 'as strong a thrust as possible towards Cassino and Frosinone shortly before the assault landing to draw in enemy reserves that might be employed against the landing forces and then to create a breach in his front through which every opportunity will be taken to link up rapidly with the seaborne operation'. Despite the switch, in all, of five divisions from Eighth Army to the Fifth Army, German resistance on the main front remained stubborn; and during the early critical days the British and United States divisions at Anzio had to fight unaided for their own salvation. Meanwhile, on the Adriatic sector, General Montgomery had continued with his attempt to break through the enemy's defensive system; but with even less success as the weather worsened and the enemy's strength increased.

Although the landing itself was unopposed, there was an initial setback. When the British 1 Division got ashore they had great difficulty in wedding-up their fighting vehicles to the troops already on land, because of the deep and heaving sand dunes. The result was that the beaches had to be abandoned for this purpose and the landing of fighting vehicles transferred to the port of Anzio, which was already heavily overcrowded by the United States 3 Division.

When I landed on the morning of the assault I saw for myself the difficulties 1 Division were having with their wheeled equipment. The switch to Port Anzio was made that evening. Before I left I felt confident that VI Corps were sufficiently established to push forward light mobile forces to gain contact with any German forces in the vicinity. But it seems that such mobile forces were not sent out in any strength until it was too late to take advantage of the surprise already gained.

Against a less formidable foe an operation such as we had devised would have succeeded; but I think we may well have under-
estimated the remarkable resilience and toughness of the Germans,
in expecting them to be frightened by such a threat to their rear.

Hitler's orders to Kesselring were to hold on to Cassino at all
costs, for political reasons, and to eliminate the Anzio landing. The
withdrawal of the Hermann Göring division from Italy was can-
celled, and Hitler told Kesselring that he would be reinforced by
two motorized divisions, three independent regiments, two heavy
tank battalions and some heavy and medium artillery units. Thus
the enemy refused to weaken his battle-front at Cassino by drawing back formations to deal with the landings.

From the map an operation based on Anzio to secure the Alban
Hills, with the object of cutting the German line of communication to Cassino, looks an attractive proposition. But when viewing
the objective from the beachhead one appreciates in better per-
spective the formidability of the task. The Alban Hills are really a
massive mountain terrain, much more difficult to gain and maintain than can be apparent from maps. And to have secured the hills
and kept open the line of communication to Anzio would not have
been an easy task.

It is of interest to consider what our position would have been if
the fresh German divisions had found us stretched from Anzio to
the Alban Hills. Could we have maintained our bridgehead intact
on such a wide perimeter with the troops at our disposal? We had
no more than two divisions. And it would have been disastrous to
our ultimate operations if Anzio had been wiped out.

As it was, the comparatively local bridgehead was held with
difficulty against extremely serious enemy counter-attacks, but
when it was secure it gave us the opportunity to reinforce our
positions at Anzio and build up a force of seven divisions.

Every time we attacked Kesselring in Italy we took him completely by surprise; but he showed very great skill in extricating
himself from the desperate situations into which his faulty Intelligence had led him. I feel now that he would not, in these
circumstances, have altered his dispositions on the main front to
any great degree until he had tried every means to eliminate the
threat to his rear. Nor need his determination be doubted. The
forces under his command had been engaged in a continuous

retreat for almost a year, since November 1942, a retreat that had brought them just short of Alexandria to just north of Naples—and it was time to put a stop to it.

However, it is often easy to find consolation when one has the inestimable advantage of wisdom after the event—and there still remains the question, what went wrong with the Anzio operation, seeing that we gained almost complete surprise?

The answer is clear. The commander of the assault corps, the American General John Lucas, missed his opportunity by being too slow and cautious. He failed to realize the great advantage that surprise had given him. He allowed time to beat him.

General Lucas was selected to command the operation because he was the only available corps commander who was not actively engaged at the time. Moreover, since Anzio was on the Fifth Army front, he was a logical choice. Salerno had been his first experience of an amphibious landing, and the going there for the first week had been pretty tough. On looking back I feel sure General Lucas expected that he would have to fight his way ashore as we did at Salerno and, in general, anticipated a repetition of that landing. On finding that he was not opposed he was taken by surprise and unable to adjust his mind to a new situation. A younger or more experienced soldier would have been quicker to react.

The whole undertaking, of course, was a risk; but it was a carefully calculated risk and had every opportunity of coming off if the operations had been handled with dash and vigour—which, as I have made clear, they were not.

As a footnote to history I would add that some time was to elapse before Mark Clark could be persuaded to relinquish the services of General Lucas—in fact, precisely one month. His appointment, of course, was entirely an American affair, and it would have been quite inappropriate for me to have intervened. However, at the last I brought myself to remark to Mark Clark:

'You know, the position is serious. We may be pushed back into the sea. That would be very bad for both of us—and you would certainly be relieved of your command.'

This gentle injunction, I am glad to say, impelled action.

A tribute is due to the work of the Royal Navy. Never once did they fail to give us soldiers all the support we demanded of them. After the surrender of the Italian naval forces in the Mediterranean, they devoted their services almost exclusively to the support and assistance of land operations. They carried two armies across the sea in the invasion of Sicily, and maintained us on the island until we were ready to invade the Italian mainland. Later they put us ashore at Salerno, and, as I have already noted, supported our troops with their gunfire when they were being heavily attacked by the Luftwaffe.

Looking back on the Anzio operation, I will recall what I wrote in my despatch: 'The Allied navies uncomplainingly accepted a burden both greater in degree and of longer duration than had been expected, and maintained a force which by May had grown to over seven divisions, through a harbour no bigger than a fishing port and under continuous fire.'

ADVANCE ON ROME

When the final battle for Rome was launched the role of the Anzio force was to break out and at Valmontone get across the German main line of supply to their troops at Cassino. But for some inexplicable reason General Clark's Anglo-American forces never reached their objectives, though, according to my information later, there was nothing to prevent their being gained. Instead, Mark Clark switched his point of attack north to the Alban Hills, in the direction of Rome.

If he had succeeded in carrying out my plan the disaster to the enemy would have been much greater; indeed, most of the German forces south of Rome would have been destroyed. True, the battle ended in a decisive victory for us, but it was not as complete as it might have been.

In my plan for the defeat of the enemy I made it clear, in the boundaries I laid down between the British Eighth Army and the United States Fifth Army, that the Americans would enter Rome and the British with their allies would by-pass it. I had always assured General Clark in conversation that Rome would be entered by his army; and I can only assume that the immediate lure of Rome for its publicity value persuaded him to switch the direction of his advance.

This episode gives me the opportunity of recalling a charming gesture on the part of General Eisenhower—in almost the last signal he sent me before leaving the Mediterranean.

The disadvantages of employing a mixed Corps are of course as obvious to you as to me. I have wondered whether or not you may have been influenced by either of the following factors: that you felt it undesirable, because of the risks involved, to hazard a Corps of two American divisions when you as a British officer have the deciding responsibility or that you may have thought it undesirable from a political viewpoint for a Corps of two British divisions to be given the opportunity for the direct capture of Rome. In my opinion neither of these factors should be allowed to outweigh the military advantages of launching your assault by any troops you believe best fitted and most available. In giving these views I merely wish to remove any political difficulties that may occur to you in order that you can launch the best military operation that can be laid on in the time available.

I replied that the composition of the Corps was based solely on the best formations at the time: 'The political aspect is of no consequence; but I do think the sharing of risks and hazards together is of importance'.

The liberation of Rome was carefully timed to take place just before the Normandy landings. The fall of this ancient capital would, it was felt, hearten the troops about to go into battle in northern France and correspondingly dishearten the enemy. Winston Churchill was as anxious over the timing of the victory as ever he had been over the defeat of the Afrika Korps at Alamein. Rome in fact fell to the Allied Armies in Italy two days before the Anglo-American invasion of France. Although the Anzio–Cassino pincer movement failed to close and encircle the enemy, the battle had been decisive enough.

The capture of Rome was agreed by the British and United States Chiefs of Staff to be of the utmost value to the Allied war effort; but it may be asked how did it fit into the whole of our strategy? Could we have stopped at Rome, for example, and remained content with the possession of the Foggia airfields for the bombing of southern Germany? The question itself misses the whole aim and object of the campaign in Italy, namely, to engage as many German divisions as possible, in order to draw them away from the main battle-front in north-west Europe.

Our success in carrying out this mission is evident from the figures; for, in all, at one time or another, forty-five German divisions were employed in Italy, together with four Italian regular divisions, one Cossack division, and miscellaneous formations of Czechs, Slovaks, and Russians. Among this number the German High Command disposed of some of their finest troops, such as the Hermann Göring Division and 1 Parachute Division that fought so gallantly at Cassino. And these German formations, though reduced in establishment, never lacked reinforcements and administrative support to keep them in the field. Thus we were not fighting rubbish.

We ourselves employed in Italy a total of forty divisions, of which eight were transferred to the United Kingdom in 1943, in readiness for the campaign in north-west Europe; ten more followed them in 1944 and 1945, while three were diverted to Greece towards the end of 1944.

Just after the capture of Rome I made my advanced headquarters in a villa at Frascati, in a small building that had been used by Field-Marshal Kesselring for the same purpose. We were there only a few days, and during our stay Field-Marshal Smuts spent a night with us. It was during this visit that he remarked, in the course of a memorable discourse: 'We are living in one of those rare epochs of history when once again we see that mankind has struck his tents and is on the march. When and where it will end we have yet to know.' These were his words as I clearly recall them. Years were to elapse before I learned that he was actually quoting from a pamphlet he had written on the League of Nations, in which, after remarking that 'mankind is once more on the move', he continued: 'The very foundations have been shaken and loosened, and things are again fluid. The tents have been struck, and the great caravan of humanity is once more on the march.' One can hardly doubt that the revised version is to be preferred.

Soon afterwards King George VI visited his armies in Italy and spent a week with me at my caravan H.Q. on the eastern shores of Lake Bolsena. Sometimes when we returned from a visit to the forward troops we got back early, and then we took strolls together along the lake. I think that the King appreciated those jaunts tremendously and he behaved as if he were on holiday. He was very relaxed and seemed to enjoy it all.

I gave him my caravan to live in. It amused me that he wasn't at all satisfied with my simple comforts, and had fresh lighting installed and a small extra tent attached to the caravan. He also brought a bath made of some sort of rubber stuff—I think it came from a barrage balloon. It was an excellent bath, and when he left he gave me it and the other things, much to my pleasure and extra comfort.

I was told that the old castle in the town of Bolsena belonged to an Englishman, but no one knew his real name—they knew him only by his Papal title. Years afterwards, when I was in Canada, I ran into a certain O'Brien ffrench: he was an Irishman who had once served, I think, in an English cavalry regiment. He now owned a ranch outside Jasper, in the Rockies.

One day when we were discussing the Italian campaign, I mentioned the name Bolsena and he told me that he had a property there which he had inherited from his father. So at last, and quite by chance, I had found the mysterious owner of the castle of whom the inhabitants of Bolsena had talked when I had my headquarters there during the war.

Of the many messages I received from Winston Churchill, two which I particularly cherish belong to this period—though I will not pretend that I greeted them with much enthusiasm at the time. The first reached me during a lull and ran something like this:

What are you doing sitting down doing nothing? Why don't you use your armour in a great scythe-like movement through the mountains?

The other came when we were bogged down at Anzio:

I expected to see a wild cat roaring into the mountains—and what do I find? A whale wallowing on the beaches!

Despite the disappointments that it brought, I never lost faith in the strategic validity of the Italian campaign, which owed virtually all its inspiration to Winston; nor did I feel any sort of regret when, because I was so close to it, he refused to release me to Ike to become his deputy in north-west Europe. I should have been more than reluctant to have taken farewell of the troops of the many nations that fought under my command in the Mediterranean.

And, anyway, I prefer command!

XI

INTERLUDE AT LAKE BOLSENA

THE RUSSIANS

IT WAS at Lake Bolsena that Bogomolov, the Russian Ambassador in Italy, paid us a visit. It was all very extraordinary. I had met Bogomolov in Rome when he was complaining of the heat and the stuffiness; so I said, 'Would you like to come to spend a week-end with me on the shores of Lake Bolsena, where I have a little tented camp?'

'Thank you so much—I would love to come,' he replied.

'Then come along,' I said, 'and bring anybody you like with you.'

In order to give him as good a time as possible I got hold of a motor-launch and had three special tents put up for him and his party. He arrived on a Saturday evening. We had dinner, and I suppose we began to move off to bed at about half past ten or eleven. I said, 'Well, shall we say breakfast tomorrow at eight?' They agreed. We all went to bed. But when, next morning, there was no sign of the Russians, I sent my A.D.C., Rupert Clarke, to see what had happened to them. He came back looking amused and pink. 'They've gone,' he said.

'Gone? They can't have gone!'

He said, 'Well, they have.'

It appeared that they didn't relish being put in three separate tents and had all crowded into one. And when he went to fetch them he found the tent completely empty. However, there was a piece of paper pinned to a pillow, and its message was something to this effect: 'So sorry. Have important work and engagements in Rome. Must return.' Just that and nothing more.

I asked our signals, 'Did the Russian Ambassador get any message last evening which might cause him to flee to Rome in the middle of the night?' No—nothing had passed through our signals. And I never had another word from Bogomolov.

MARSHAL TITO

Marshal Tito also paid us a visit; he flew from Belgrade to discuss his operations against the Germans in Yugoslavia. At this time I was helping him with food, medical supplies, and artillery, and in addition the R.A.F. had lent him a unit.

There was an oak tree just outside the mess tent, above Lake Bolsena, and we sat beneath it and discussed our mutual affairs. This was my first meeting with Tito, and I was very impressed with him. He was a fine and very friendly man, and he told me about his difficulties with the Germans. I was able to do more for him when I knew precisely what were his requirements. I was to meet him again just after Yalta; and in the last days of the war in Italy I was again to encounter the Marshal—though not in person—in less happy circumstances, on the road to Trieste, when the future of that city rested on a razor edge.

When I went to see the Marshal after Yalta I fancy that I expressed a wish, to the Russian military representative in Belgrade, that I might meet Marshal Tolbukhin in order to see if we could usefully co-ordinate our operational plans. Arrangements were quickly made and I flew from Belgrade in a Russian aircraft—which, incidentally, I was allowed to pilot myself. We landed near a small Hungarian town and went by car to Marshal Tolbukhin's headquarters, which struck me as looking very newly set up and lacking the activity of an Army Group headquarters.

I was shown to my billet, a small and comfortable little house in the village, where a Russian girl was detailed to look after me, as a sort of female valet, I suppose. She wore a dress or uniform vaguely reminiscent of that of a hospital nurse. It appeared that she intended to sleep on the settee in my room, but I didn't think that was quite the thing, and she spent the night outside the door.

My knowledge of the Russian language is not extensive, but it is sufficient for conversation. So, talking to her, I asked when Russian headquarters had been set up in that village. 'Yesterday,' she said. My suspicions were confirmed: it was not an Army Group H.Q. at all, but a temporary installation specially set up to receive me.

Presumably the Russians didn't wish me to know where their Army Group H.Q. was.

I was received by Marshal Tolbukhin with all the hospitality for which the Russians are famous. He was an elderly man, heavily built—certainly an impressive figure. Colonel-General Jeltof, his chief of staff, never left the Marshal's side and sat next to him at dinner. I surmised, correctly as it turned out, that he was the political commissar.

Before dinner I had a private discussion with the Marshal about our respective operations and intentions. Our plans were subjected to the keenest inquiry but he was not very forthcoming about his own. I asked him about his powers in the conduct of operations. He told me that an objective would be given to him in a directive from Moscow, and that the necessary extra formations would be sent to him, administered by Moscow, and maintained from home. All he had to do was to prepare the plan of battle and direct the operations. When the objective had been gained the supplementary shock troops were withdrawn from him. Centralized control of the battle-front could hardly go farther.

Just before dinner, when we were left alone for a moment or two, the Marshal noticed that among my medal ribbons I had the old Tsarist Order of St. Anne with crossed swords. As he put his finger on it he sighed, 'I have that, too, but I'm not allowed to wear it.' During the First World War, Marshal Tolbukhin (he died in 1949) had commanded a battalion in the old Imperial Army.

STALIN

I met Stalin for the first time at the Yalta conference, in February 1945. He was much smaller than I had been led to believe from the photographs I had seen of him. His complexion was yellow and blotchy, and his grizzled hair, though thick in front, was thin on the top of his head. His small, dark eyes had a distinct twinkle when he was in a good humour and making jokes; but he could look extremely formidable when he was serious or displeased. I never saw him in any other than military dress.

In those days Winston Churchill carried with him, on his journeys overseas, a map-room of the battle-fronts, set up by a staff officer. I was in this map-room one day with the Prime Minister, Stalin, an interpreter, and the staff officer, when

Churchill asked Stalin to indicate the situation on the Russian front and give us some idea of his future plans. The Generalissimo obliged by offering what I thought was a very vague indication of his projected offensives. Whether he knew as much about the military plans of the Russian armies as we had been led to believe, or whether he was not prepared to reveal them, is open to conjecture.

Stalin made one significant reply to a question put to him by the Prime Minister. He said: 'We have already lost four million soldiers on the field of battle, and the war is not yet won—and they are human beings, you know.'

Four million dead! It was so. When I got back to my headquarters in Italy I asked for the War Office estimate of the Russian losses up to date, and the answer was, 'Anything up to four and a half million.'

XII

THE CRUEL MOUNTAINS

THE GOTHIC LINE

THE German retreat from Rome to the north was rapid and, inevitably, disorganized. The roads along which we harried their retreating forces were littered with burnt-out and abandoned vehicles, destroyed by our air force or by our armoured pursuit, or left by their drivers when fuel ran out. Except for some strong rearguard actions at Poggibonsi and Lake Trasimene—two key-positions on the enemy guard-line between Leghorn and Rimini—my Fifteenth Army Group reached the River Arno with very little delay.

The Germans made no attempt to hold the line of the Arno. At Florence—more as a gesture of defiance than anything else—they blew all the bridges, with the exception of the picturesque Ponte Vecchio; nevertheless, they destroyed or mined the houses at both ends of the bridge, in a feeble and certainly futile attempt to create some sort of obstacle to our advance. It is pleasant to be able to record that the Italians have now restored all the bridges—using the original stones, retrieved from the river.

Those who have never seen the Apennines in Italy cannot hope to appreciate the formidable obstacle they present to a force advancing from the south. This great range of mountains, rising to nearly seven thousand feet, stretches across the peninsula from the Mediterranean to the Adriatic. To the south of this great barrier the mountains tumble into foothills as far as the River Arno.

For over a year the Todt labour organization had been working for Hitler on the construction of a line—the Gothic Line—a highly developed series of strongpoints stretching for about two hundred miles across the peninsula, from Spezia on the

135

Ligurian Sea, to Pesaro, south of Rimmi, on the Adriatic. The Line blocked every route north. Such was the military prospect facing the Fifteenth Army Group towards the end of the summer of 1944, when the enemy had been driven back north of the Arno.

It was now that I lost seven divisions—three United States and four French—from my Fifteenth Army Group; they went to form the invasion force for the strategically useless attack on the South of France. But in spite of the weakening of my forces by the withdrawal of so much splendid fighting material, the Fifteenth Army Group performed a feat of military prowess which surely has never been surpassed.

The Gothic Line was stormed by the United States Fifth Army and the British Eighth Army. Both attacks were initially successful. The Fifth Army seized the Futa Pass, a key-point in the Gothic Line, while the Greek Mountain Brigade, under command of Canadian 1 Division, entered Rimini on 21 September. The Futa Pass is at the highest point of the road over the Apennines; from it there is a magnificent view over the peaks as far as the Po Valley.

The Americans had performed a magnificent feat of arms against a brave and stubborn enemy; but on reaching the top of the pass any sense of elation must have been short-lived in face of the many miles of rugged mountains that still barred the way before they could reach the level of the Po Valley. Moreover, the Germans, as always, fought to retain every inch of the ground they still held.

Thus by the end of September the Gothic Line had been completely turned by the Eighth Army—it had advanced some thirty miles in twenty-six days—and pierced at its centre; and the enemy abandoned such of the prepared positions as still remained in his hands except for a small sector in the extreme west.

The Allied Armies in Italy had won a great success, though at high cost. Eighth Army casualties alone had been fourteen thousand men—higher than for Alamein—and two hundred and ten tanks had been lost. The tanks were easily replaceable; the men were not. Nor would the success be easy to exploit. It had been confidently expected that, after breaking into the flat expanse of the Romagna, we should be able to stage a rapid advance to the Po; but the continuous water-lines of the Romagna and of the Po Valley itself were to prove hardly less serious obstacles than the mountains over which we had fought. Soon the 'rushing streams of summer' were to become the raging torrents of an 'abominable' autumn; and although by mid-October both the Fifth and the Eighth Armies were within a day or so's march of their goals— Bologna and Ravenna—it was shortly obvious that final destruction of the German armies in Italy would have to be postponed until the spring of 1945.

About this time I had a visit from the Prime Minister. Winston was always bothering me to take him up to the front to see a battle, and so far I had dodged his requests because a trip would have been too much of a risk. But now he was more insistent than ever, and I thought, well, after all, we have practically won the war at last. So, when we were advancing, I took him in a jeep close behind the assault troops.

What really frightened me was that we were going over ground which hadn't been swept for mines, and in addition shells and stray bullets were whizzing around. But I got him safely to a farm-house overlooking a valley.

We could hear the machine-guns of the infantry going rat-tat-tat-tat just below us; and on the hill in front, which couldn't have been more than 1,200 yards away, our tanks were creeping up under the ridge, advancing a little, then firing and coming back, to duck the German anti-tank gun fire, which their action had drawn. Winston saw it all like a demonstration, and was as happy as the proverbial sand-boy.

About this time, too, through our Intelligence, we gained information that the Germans had a project with the codename 'Herbst Nebel'—'Autumn Mist'. Now we knew that the Germans were not in any position to carry out an offensive of major importance, if only because we were holding all the commanding features in the Apennines. What were they up to?

It was an easy problem. As the valley of the Po is famous for its autumn fogs, it was not difficult to guess that the codename referred to a plan to withdraw their troops into the valley. However, the project was to remain nothing but a codename: it took no account of the fact that 'retreat' was a word not included in the Führer's military vocabulary. Yet the affair illustrates the danger of having a secret codeword with a built-in clue to its meaning.

THE ROAD TO VIENNA

Once in full possession of the Po Valley, I could strike in several directions. North and west I should be faced by the formidable barrier of the Alps, but to the north-east lay less rugged country, and once through the so-called Ljubljana Gap the way led to Vienna, an objective of great political and psychological value. And I should have had an excellent base in Trieste from which to conduct operations, with my right flank considerably reinforced by the Yugoslav resistance forces under Marshal Tito.

The terrain between Trieste and the Drava river is mountainous, but not more so than much of Italy over which we had advanced successfully; and troops which could overcome a brave and stubborn enemy such as we had met in the Apennine ranges north of Florence would surely not be stopped by what we might find in Yugoslavia and beyond.

It was a dazzling idea, this grand project of reaching Vienna before our Russian allies, and we discussed it informally at my headquarters. Yet it would have been premature to start planning such an operation before it was certain that we could reach the valley of the Po before the end of 1944. As events turned out, we did not reach the Po that winter, although we were not far from it.

Operation 'Dragoon'—which I have already touched on in my comments on General Eisenhower's views on the strategy of the western war—was to remain in the balance almost until its own particular D Day on 15 August 1944. On the assumption that it might still not go ahead, I called a conference of my army commanders on 23 June, and explained what my plans would be if I were assured the same forces as were then available to me.

The object of operations in Italy must be to invade southern Germany by an overland advance through north-eastern Italy and the Ljubljana Gap. By this means we should strike directly at territory that it was vital for the Germans to defend, even at the cost of diverting strength from other fronts; we should also have the possibility of joining hands with the southern wing of the Red Army and with Marshal Tito's partisan forces. The alternative, an advance into southern France across the Maritime Alps, would be less profitable and more difficult. I appreciated that the enemy intended to hold the northern Apennines until driven from the position in overwhelming force; but, with the troops then available to him, he would certainly fail and risk disaster, provided we could bring our whole strength against him.

The decision by the Combined Chiefs of Staff to go forward with 'Dragoon' was taken a little more than a week later although, as I have already related, Mr. Churchill was to continue the argument until within five days of the launching of the operation. It reached me on 2 July—together with the intimation that I was to lose still more troops and that my air strength would be reduced probably by seventy per cent! My task was to remain—'the destruction of the German forces in Italy'.

So faded the last hope of a spectacular development of the campaign in Italy. I am thoroughly aware that it had taken us ten months to push forward three hundred and fifty miles from Salerno to Rimini and Florence, and that Vienna lay twice that distance ahead. Nevertheless, without overlooking the time and space factors, and without discounting the obstacles favourable to a delaying defence—which, incidentally, would have been right up the line of country of Tito's guerrillas—I shall always believe that the Allied Armies in Italy would have gone forward with a new impetus at the prospect of a wider victory. Instead—as I had to note in my despatch—the state of indecision had a lowering effect on the morale and efficiency of the troops during the lost summer months of 1944.

The invasion of southern France was an American inspiration. Churchill was entirely against it; so was Alanbrooke; but since the forces engaged were all American or American-equipped, our allies had the last say. Thus my seven divisions were duly withdrawn from the Fifteenth Army Group to take part in the invasion of southern France—an operation which contributed nothing to the final victory. General de Gaulle, on his last visit to my headquarters in Italy, said to me: 'I am very sorry to take away your French Corps. General Juin and his troops have been very happy under you, but you mustn't deny Frenchmen this opportunity of taking part in the liberation of their native soil.'

In these circumstances I could not argue the matter. I would add that Marshal Juin was a professional soldier whose early service had been spent in French North Africa. During the First World War he was seriously wounded in the right arm, and it is for this reason that he always salutes with his left. He was a very fine commander indeed, as his record bears witness.

Apart from the New Zealanders, who were, *par excellence*, the exploiters of a favourable opening on the battlefield, the French Corps were the quickest to take advantage of any weak spot in the enemy's defences. The Corps, of course, was afterwards to fight with General de Lattre de Tassigny's French First Army—later to be christened the Army of the Rhine and Danube. But I have a feeling that it might have achieved a greater glory had it marched on Vienna instead of undertaking a somewhat circuitous advance to the Upper Danube, inside Germany, by way of the Côte d'Azur.

XIII

CRISIS IN GREECE

ON 12 December 1944 I took over as Supreme Allied Commander, Mediterranean Forces, from General Wilson; and just before taking up my appointment I was called to London to see the Prime Minister and the Chief of the Imperial General Staff.

At my interview with him Winston Churchill said: 'I am not at all happy over the situation which is developing in Greece. As soon as you return to Italy I want you to go at once to Athens and find out what is happening. Deal with the situation as you think fit, but keep me closely informed.'

I spent one night at Supreme Allied H.Q. in Caserta, and the following day flew to Athens with Harold Macmillan, my political adviser. The first thing we learned was that the Communist-inspired ELAS-EAM—respectively the military and the political wings of the Greek liberation movement—had already seized the port of Piracus and surrounded—though without attacking—the airport. When I asked for a motor-car to take me to our military headquarters in Athens I was told that I should need an armoured-car, since ELAS-EAM were in occupation of the area between the airport and Athens. And all the telephone exchanges were in Communist hands.

Not a very happy welcome! However, the Communists obligingly put through my call to the commander of our troops in Athens, General Ronald Scobie, who by now had some 5,000 men at his disposal, and in due time two armoured-cars arrived to take us the six or seven miles to Athens. We bought a lot of bullets on the journey—we could hear them hitting the outside of my armoured-car—but we were not stopped.

When I arrived at General Scobie's headquarters, which were almost next door to the Grande Bretagne hotel in Constitution Square, I learnt that the Communists were in control of most of the city, and that only the centre, an area which embraced British Military headquarters and the British Embassy, was still in our hands. It also appeared that all the dumps of supplies were spread about between Athens and the airport, and that they were only loosely under our control.

I was told that we had only three days' supply of ammunition and six days' supply of food. Immediate action was necessary, and I ordered General Scobie to gather in all the supplies he could to some central area safely under his control, make sure that the airport was firmly in our possession, and consolidate the position remaining to us in Athens and prevent any further incursion.

Then I sent a telegram ordering a division to fly in, at the earliest possible moment, from my forces in Italy. These fresh troops were to regain control of the port, link up with the airport, and clear up the local situation. From this firm base, operations could then be safely conducted to clear the whole of Athens of the Communists.

That same night I spent with the British Ambassador, Mr. Reginald Leeper—afterwards Sir Reginald—who was pretty well besieged in his Embassy; in fact, a bullet was fired through the window of the room in which I was sitting with Mr. Macmillan and our Ambassador.

Next morning I left for Italy, leaving Mr. Macmillan behind to sort out the political situation. It was necessary for me to get back as soon as possible to arrange a strong military set-up in Greece. General Scobie was a fine man and very popular with the Greeks: whenever he went out into the streets he was acclaimed as 'Scompoo! Scompoo!' But I don't think he appreciated the dangers of the situation as it had developed. To strengthen his staff, I therefore sent one of my best young staff officers, Brigadier Hugh Mainwaring, to act as his chief of staff. I also sent X Corps H.Q., under General Hawkesworth, to take operational command of the troops. Scobie was retained as the overall commander because of his high standing among the Greeks. Once these arrangements had been effected, the military situation rapidly improved.

The political situation, however, remained obscure. There was no strong central authority in Greece at this time, and not until the King of Greece could be induced to hand over his authority to a Regent would a solution be in sight.

It was Mr. Macmillan who advanced the claims of Archbishop Damaskinos, Archbishop of Athens. Here was a man who had refused to knuckle under to the German invader. He was a strong character, fearless and incorruptible, and as much respected by the Germans as by the Greeks: in his youth he had been a famous wrestler, and his physique was still magnificent. He was to prove a great friend of Britain. I surmised at the time that the Prime Minister was unlikely to approve of him, since he would consider that his sympathies inclined too much to the Left.

The Prime Minister arrived in Athens on Christmas Day 1944, with Anthony Eden. They stayed on board *Ajax*—the famous light cruiser of the River Plate battle—and a meeting with the Archbishop was arranged for the following day.

Churchill was sitting on a sofa when the Archbishop was ushered into the room. I think that the Prime Minister had in his mind that he was going to meet a politically sleek cleric and a man of little real importance. I happened to be in the room at the time, and I watched the encounter with fascination. Winston, slumped on the sofa, looked bored and obviously dubious about the prospects of the meeting. Then a magnificent figure of a man appeared in the doorway—strong, virile, well over six feet, with his black beard and his great head-dress which made him look like a giant.

Churchill rose in astonishment, obviously immensely impressed by the appearance of his guest. They sat down together and started a discussion which had to be interpreted. I recollect that the Prime Minister said something to which the Archbishop objected, and from that moment it was never in doubt that his Beatitude had very strong views of his own. Winston, in short, had found his man— thanks to Harold Macmillan.

It was agreed that a further conference should be called for the next day in the Greek Foreign Office; and it was allowed to get out that this conference would be held in the Grande Bretagne Hotel. The deception was wise, since a bomb was discovered under the hotel, placed there to blow us all up.

When revisiting recently the Foreign Office in Athens I recognized the conference room at once: I well recollect the big round table at which we sat, and the hurricane lamps—the electricity was not functioning because of the fighting in the city. Archbishop Damaskinos took the chair, and apart from the British contingent there were two representatives of ELAS-EAM, the French Ambassador, and a Russian. Our main purpose was to seek a stable

143

Greek Government. Nothing was decided, however, and we left the Archbishop to carry on talks with ELAS-EAM. These talks continued for several days and resulted in the acceptance of Archbishop Damaskinos as Regent and of General Plastiras, the exiled Republican leader, as Prime Minister. On 11 January a military truce was signed with ELAS-EAM, under which the guerrillas were to be disarmed, an amnesty declared, and all hostages returned. So ended another unfortunate episode in the war and our second intervention in Greece.

Nevertheless, it ended more happily than the story of our first intervention in 1941 which, I have always been given to understand, delayed the German attack on Russia by six weeks—a delay that gave the snows of Mother Russia time to get busy and help save Moscow from the invader.

But, quite recently, through diplomatic channels, I received from Colonel-General Fritz Halder, Chief of the German General Staff at the time, his own studied consideration of this widely-held belief. According to General Halder, ten German divisions were originally allocated to Grecian Thrace and a few of the north Ægean islands as a protective screen for the vital Roumanian oil bases. Though this allocation interfered with the General Staff's order of assembly for the attack on Russia it did not disrupt it, since units earmarked for the Balkans could be sent on later to join the Eastern troop assembly as army reserves after they had completed their Balkan task. General Halder continues:

When, however, in the April of 1941, British ground forces landed in Greece and clearly proposed to advance northward to join up with Yugoslavia, with whom we were now at war, the operational objective had to be changed: this was now to isolate Yugoslavia and to occupy the whole of Greece (including Crete), and thus finally to protect the eastern flank of the proposed Eastern offensive. Additional forces (including mobile forces) were to be withdrawn from the Eastern troop assembly. It was impossible to estimate exactly the time required for operations in Greece, since these depended on the strength and command of the British contingent. The German General Staff therefore advised Hitler that the advance against Russia planned for mid-May might have to be postponed for six weeks.

This deliberately over-cautious estimate was not borne out by events. Since the British were unable to bring in Turkey, and since they were clearly only intent on saving their forces, German operations through-out the whole of Greece were carried out with film-like precision, surprisingly quickly and with only negligible losses. Soon after the start of the attack the General Staff were able to withdraw a considerable part of this Balkan operational force and to incorporate it in the Eastern troop assembly.

The withdrawal, resting, and incorporation of the units needed to clear up the whole of Greece took until the beginning of June, that is, three weeks after the original date set for the Eastern offensive. This delay was of no importance to Headquarters, since the units from Greece arrived in the East in plenty of time to enable them to be used as reserves for the German Eastern Army. However, the spring floods of 1941 did not permit final plans for the offensive to be completed before mid-June. The actual date was 22 June. By then the completed Balkan operations presented no difficulties to the German H.Q.

Whichever way we look at it, our willingness to send troops to Greece, at a time when we could ill afford to weaken our forces in the Middle East, showed our readiness to aid an old friend and ally.

XIV

VICTORY IN ITALY

-

B Y April 1945 we were nearly out of the tunnel of the long, dark years; and now was the moment for the final offensive in Italy.

After I lost seven divisions to the invasion force for the attack on the south of France, I was left with seventeen divisions, four Italian combat groups, and six armoured and four infantry brigades, as against twenty-three German and four Italian (German-equipped) divisions. I enjoyed, however, almost complete control of the air.

Divisions, of course, do not provide a sound basis for comparing the strengths of opposing armies because of variations in establishments; nor indeed does the official figure of over a million and a half as the total Allied strength at this period serve as a basis of comparison with the German strength. Despite withdrawals, this figure was hardly to alter to the end of the campaign.

During the last month of the fighting the German strength in Italy, as reported in the last return rendered, on 9 April, was 439,344—fighting troops to the last man—plus 160,180 Italians: thus giving the Allies a paper superiority of nearly three to one. But the statistical approach is only half the story. It would be invidious to suggest what proportion of the Allied troops were front-line fighting soldiers; what proportion of them were fit only for occupation and security duties; and what proportion of them, through lack of training or of equipment, could be expected to undertake more than minor tasks; nor will I attempt to estimate the great hordes of civilian workers who bumped up the figure for my ration strength.

The record of the comparative casualties gives a more reliable picture. On the German side they amounted in all to 536,000; Allied casualties were 312,000. The difference is the more remarkable in that we were always the attackers. Four times we carried out the most difficult operation of war, an amphibious landing; three times we launched a prepared offensive with the full strength of an army group; nowhere in Europe did soldiers face a more difficult terrain or more determined adversaries.

Anyway, in its last offensive, the performance of the Fifteenth Army Group was the more meritorious in the light of the pre-1939 thesis that, as the result of the fire-power of modern weapons in the defence, no attack could hope to succeed without a minimum numerical superiority of three to one. In the Normandy campaign, we are told, Allied attacks hardly ever succeeded unless the attacking troops enjoy a superiority of more than five to one. Perhaps, therefore, the Allied chiefs of staff are not to be reproached for having shown so little compunction in cutting down my armies in Italy to the absolute minimum; for as Winston Churchill revealed—though not until victory was won—they had all along proceeded on the assumption that no final attack could be successfully mounted on the Italian front.

The final offensive was a resumption of the battle of the previous winter—which had been sustained specifically as a direct contribution to General Eisenhower's own winter campaign on the Western Front, despite all the difficulties of climate and terrain, of deficient man-power and material. The enemy was still on the same defence line and had been forbidden, by a Führer Order, to make even the smallest withdrawal. But the weather was now dry and favourable; and our troops, though diminished in numbers, were thoroughly rested. Indeed, the speed and weight of their blows were such that the Germans were never able to occupy any of their prepared alternative positions.

The problem for Fifth Army was to break out of the mountains where they had been dolorously locked up since the previous winter; the obstacles facing Eighth Army were, as in the previous winter, a series of water barriers and the defences based on them. In particular, the road to Ferrara, the Eighth Army's axis of advance, was narrowed to a heavily fortified causeway by extensive artificial flooding in the area of the town of Argenta. This causeway, known to us as the Argenta Gap, loomed large in our appreciations: in order to advance rapidly to the necessary crossing sites on the Po, we must either force it or outflank it. In the event we forced it—as the less difficult and less time-wasting of the two courses open to us.

The offensive started with Eighth Army's attack on the enemy's left on 9 April. It first successfully circumnavigated the waterways of the Adriatic sector of the front; then steadily progressed into the valley of the Po. The United States Fifth Army began its drive on Bologna five days later. It had still to fight bitterly through the last remaining barrier of the Apennine mountain chain.

For a week the Germans fought fanatically for every inch of the ground they held. But they were ultimately forced from their last foothold in the mountains, to find themselves in the low ground of the Po, and quite unable to re-form any coherent line of defence.

Hitler's suicidal orders of no withdrawal anywhere at any time were soon to spell disaster for his armies in Italy. The Fifteenth Army Group was now attacking their centre and beginning to envelop their left flank; organized resistance collapsed against our strongly directed offensive.

Bologna fell on 21 April: it was entered simultaneously by the Poles of Eighth Army and II Corps of Fifth Army. On the evening of the next day the Americans reached the Po River at San Benedetto, and on the 23rd Eighth Army moved up to the river in strength on either side of Ferrara. Between them these two converging thrusts had trapped thousands of German prisoners, the number of which was to mount to embarrassing proportions.

From the Po northwards, it was a pursuit pressed with the utmost vigour and gallantry against an enemy who had received a mortal blow and been deprived of all his heavy weapons and equipment; but who, nevertheless, still fought back at every opportunity, with the same determination and skill that he had shown throughout the whole campaign. Thus I was faced by a brave and skilful enemy who was still strong in divisions, which had been kept up to fighting strength.

This last battle in Italy was a text-book military operation which, by first enveloping the enemy's left wing in a classical outflanking manoeuvre and then breaking through, with a sudden blow, his weakened centre, drove him against the Po, where he was annihilated.

By 2 May an army of over half a million men had been destroyed and on that day all the enemy forces in Italy and Austria laid down their arms in unconditional surrender. Two days later, on the morning of 4 May, units of the United States Fifth Army were to join up at Vipiteno, on the Italian side of the Brenner Pass, with a column of the United States Seventh Army, advancing from Salzburg.

The instrument of surrender had been signed at my head-quarters in Caserta on 29 April 1945. The negotiations were very capably handled by General Sir William Morgan, who had suc-ceeded John Harding as my chief of staff when I became Supreme Allied Commander, Mediterranean. He had been my chief staff officer at Dunkirk. In October 1945, when I left the Mediterranean theatre, he was to succeed me in the supreme command.

The opening moves of the surrender took place as early as February 1945, when General Karl Wolff, commander of all the SS in Italy, got into contact with Mr. Allen Dulles, brother of the late John Foster Dulles. Allen Dulles, destined one day to become Chief of the United States Central Intelligence Agency, was then in Switzerland. Shortly after their secret negotiations began, Field-Marshal Kesselring was transferred from Italy to north-west Europe. General von Vietinghoff succeeded him, and the secret negotiations were resumed.

The task of keeping in touch with the new C.-in-C. of the Ger-man forces in Italy devolved upon a German-speaking Czech known to us as 'Little Wally', who was working for the American O.S.S. (Office of Strategic Services). He had been a law student in Prague when the Germans invaded his country, and had joined the Czech underground movement; but he was captured and im-prisoned in Dachau. Now, after many tribulations, his moment had come. In the uniform of an SS lieutenant he was sent to General Wolff's headquarters in Milan, where he worked a wireless set at the top of the house. No one other than Wolff and his chief of staff knew of its existence.

Before the final arrangements for the capitulation could be com-pleted, the news was released of Hitler's death; and General von Vietinghoff at once sent out orders to his troops to lay down their arms. These orders took effect just an hour before the time agreed on for the surrender.

General von Vietinghoff, like most of the senior German gene-rals, was an able commander who reacted with speed and determination when faced with a dangerous situation. During the whole campaign, the German ability to switch forces quickly from one part of the front to a threatened area was remarkable, and was largely responsible for saving the enemy from many a dangerous situation.

Today the tremendous fire-power of modern weapons, when concentrated, makes possible the blowing of a hole in the enemy's defences. To take advantage of this initial success it is necessary to exploit it before the enemy can seal in the attackers. The Germans were masters of these tactics of blocking and holding on to key-points until they could bring their reserves into action. These tactics, to achieve success, require very rapid movement; and, of course, bravery and toughness in defence, since a few men or a small scratch group may have to hang on to a key-point in isolation.

Such exceptional tactical manoeuvrability is best countered by exerting pressure on as broad a front as possible, and in sufficient strength to pin down the enemy, while retaining on the main axis of attack the necessary resources to ensure counter-penetration and its exploitation. These two requirements are, of course, conflicting, and the art is to hold a proper balance between them.

After the surrender I visited prisoners of war to satisfy myself that their treatment was in accordance with those rules of conduct which we as a nation consider right and proper.

Before I visited General von Vietinghoff a reminiscence of the aftermath of the First World War prompted me to see that he was informed that it was not the British custom to shake hands with one's former opponent, bearing in mind that the surrender had taken place only a few days previously. Personally, I think that this procedure is not only correct but wise, remembering as I do the embarrassment caused by an incident which occurred in the Baltic in 1919. It was like this.

General Sir Hubert Gough and General von der Goltz met in a log cabin, mid-way between Riga and Mittau, to discuss the arrangements for the withdrawal of all the German forces from Latvia and Lithuania, in accordance with the terms of the armistice. When General Gough came into the room he held out his hand in greeting; von der Goltz bowed politely but kept his hands behind his back. It was not a very good beginning to their discussions, and a great deal of ill feeling resulted from this slight to Gough. After the conference, however, General von der Goltz had this message conveyed to General Gough:

I have nothing but respect for the British General Gough, but I Cannot bring myself to shake the hand of the representative of a country which is demanding the extradition of my Kaiser.

Anyway, when von Vietinghoff and I met we bowed to each other, and I asked him if he had any complaints about his accommodation and treatment or if there was anything he needed. He hesitated before saying that he would appreciate some green vegetables. His wish was granted at once.

Von Vietinghoff, who was never on the list of war criminals, was freed in due course, and he went to live with his family in retirement. A few years later, when I was Governor-General of Canada, I received a letter from the general's wife: she said that their old nannie, who had been with the family for more than twenty years, was required to leave them and return to Silesia, behind the Iron Curtain, because of a recent order in the American zone of occupation decreeing the repatriation of all German citizens to the place of their birth. Since it was clear that the old nurse really was one of the family, I didn't hesitate to write to the Commandant of the U.S. zone, asking him if he couldn't make the rule about repatriation sufficiently elastic to deal with a problem of this sort. I am glad to say that he was able to intervene.

General von Vietinghoff was a fair and honourable opponent. I saw him only once, and I should have been pleased to meet him again when I returned from Canada in 1952 to become Minister of Defence in Winston Churchill's Cabinet. He died, however, just before I left for home.

In our tentative planning for a move on Vienna, via the Ljubljana Gap, to forestall the Russians, the port of Trieste was essential as a firm base into which we could feed our seaborne supplies, supplemented by what could be carried overland. In passing, I would remark that a military base must be owned, administered, and completely under the control of the commander of the force using it. It is not good enough to be allowed to use it on sufferance; nor can it be shared by an ally, no matter how co-operative he may wish to be.

I knew that the Yugoslavs had a strong underground resistance organization ready to seize Trieste when the Germans were weak enough to be overcome, or, perhaps, when they were preparing to evacuate it. Accordingly I ordered General Freyberg, who commanded that splendid New Zealand division, to ignore any remaining enemy resistance or threat to his flanks immediately the German front was broken in the Po Valley and to drive on Trieste with all speed.

In the event, Tito's troops entered Trieste on 30 April, hoping not only to secure the city and the surrounding area, but also to obtain the surrender of the German garrison of 7,000 men with all its equipment. Not until the afternoon of the following day did the Yugoslav forces make contact with the advance guard of the New Zealand 2 Division just west of Monfalcon—itself some thirty miles west of Trieste. Nevertheless, on 2 May General Freyberg and his New Zealand troops entered the city, took the surrender of the German garrison, and occupied the dock areas. However, Marshal Tito's brave resistance organization continued to lay claim to Trieste: a situation that was not to be sorted out till long after the war.

So ended the Italian campaign, exactly twenty months to the day from the date when our forces landed on the peninsula. The Allied main armies in Italy were not engaged with the enemy's main armies and their attacks were not directed, as were those of the Allies in the west or the Russians in the east, against the heart of the German Fatherland and the nerve-centres of Germany's national existence; but I would again emphasize that in the summer of 1944, the crisis of the war, the Germans found themselves forced to divert eight divisions to this secondary theatre. It was then that our subordinate and preparatory role paid off. At that time, when the value of our strategic contribution was at its greatest, fifty-five German divisions were tied down in the Mediterranean by the threat, actual or potential, presented by our armies in Italy; that is, twenty-five in Italy, eleven in the south of France, and nineteen in the Balkans. In particular, there can be no doubt at all that the indirect effect of our menacing position in Italy resulted in this diversion of Germany's limited strength to guard her Balkan flank.

I say again—and it was on this note that I concluded my last despatch—I do not doubt that the campaign in Italy fulfilled its strategic mission. The soldiers, sailors, and airmen of so many nationalities who fought in Italy never had the pleasure of a conquering advance into the heart of Germany; they had none of the obvious targets before them that buoyed up their comrades on the Western Front, but only one more mountain range to cross in the face of an enemy resistance that never seemed to weaken. Perhaps not many of them realized how vital was the part they played; but all could feel pride in the way in which they played it and in the sense of duty well performed.

XV

LAST PARADE

GREAT armies in the field, if they are successful in battle, contrive to have fine commanders: some better than others, no doubt, but all worthy of the laurels that victory bestows. Of this select number is General Freyberg, who made his name in the First World War and greatly enhanced his reputation in the second. He had been wounded so many times in action that Winston Churchill dubbed him 'the Empire's Salamander'.

His New Zealand division—my *Corps de Chasse*, though, I regret to say, it had to be dissolved as a corps in March 1943 after the gruelling Cassino battles—was a great fighting formation which played an outstanding role in the Western Desert campaign and again in Italy. The story is that, on the way to Trieste, his men advanced with even more than their usual impetus because they knew that their general had spent his honeymoon at the Hotel Danieli in Venice, and were determined to requisition it for him!

Many factors contribute to victory. But whatever an army may have—weapons, equipment, material resources of all kinds—it will not count for much if the right men are lacking.

General John Harding was certainly the right man—he came to me as my chief of staff in Italy in January 1944, after having been through most of the desert campaign, where he ended up in command of the famous Desert Rats in the victorious advance that followed the battle of Alamein. He was severely wounded just before the capture of Tripoli, and had been on convalescence in England, where he had held command of a corps. I was fortunate to have such a fine soldier and capable staff officer, and, besides, a delightful companion who was liked and trusted by all the many nationalities that composed my armies during the Mediterranean campaign. When I handed over command of the Fifteenth Army Group to General Mark Clark and became Supreme Allied Commander, I gave General Harding command of XIII Corps, a formation which was directed by him with great dash and gallantry in the final offensive in Italy.

General Anders was another of my successful corps commanders. He had been a cavalry officer in the Russian Army during the First World War, but he fought with the Polish armed forces in 1940 against the Russian invader. He had a great fighting corps of gallant Polish soldiers, whose performance was unexcelled by that of any other corps under my command, and he led them with considerable distinction. He always managed to keep his corps up to strength and, indeed, over strength.

Then one day he came to me and said: 'General, I'm in trouble. You know I'm only allowed an establishment of a hundred thousand men, but my strength now is 120,000.' This was astonishing news in view of the Poles' heavy battle casualties. When I asked him how he had contrived to find these volunteers, he explained that from the large number of prisoners the corps had taken, he had recruited many soldiers, who preferred to fight on our side rather than with the enemy. A number of them were indeed Poles who had been swept up into the German Army and compelled to fight for the Germans. I am glad that I was able to reward his spirit of enterprise by making the necessary arrangements for the accommodation of this unusual accession of strength to the Polish Corps.

Twenty-six nations contributed contingents to my command in Italy. Since we are unlikely to see such an array again take the field under one command—and for the benefit of the sceptical!—I will list them. The major partners, of course, were British and American; the others—Canadian, New Zealand, South African, Newfoundland, Indian, Singhalese, Basuto, Swazi, Bechuana, Seychellois, Mauritian, Rodriguez Islanders, Caribbean, Cypriot, French, Polish, Nepalese, Belgian, Greek, Brazilian, Syro-Lebanese, Jewish, Yugoslav, Italian.

I feel, therefore, it will be agreed that I speak from first-hand experience of the varying fighting qualities of troops in battle when I affirm that there are no better soldiers than those of the British race, provided they have a cause worth fighting for—and dying for, if necessary.

They object to being pushed around—they are intelligent enough to want to know what it is all about and they will become unhappy and disgruntled if they feel that unfairness exists. Yet, if their leaders are worthy of them, they will follow them anywhere. They are very patient and tough in defence. Yet though the British will go into the attack with great bravery and tenacity, as a whole they are not quick to exploit a success or to react to a sudden emergency.

British military leaders are reluctant to accept heavy losses unless the scales of victory are weighted in their favour. This attitude of mind no doubt results from our experiences in the First World War, when our enormous casualties in such battles as the Somme and Passchendaele gave us nothing more than a few square miles of French territory, and sometimes achieved an advance of no more than a few yards.

Apart from the Irishman, who is apt to be temperamental and requires careful handling, I could never detect any marked difference, from the military point of view, between the various regional contingents which together formed the British Army.

And what of the foe that our soldiers and those of our allies overcame and mastered? Having fought against the Germans in two world wars, and with them in a minor one when I was commanding the Baltic Landwehr in 1919–20, I cannot conceal my regard for their ability as fighting men. They are very brave and tough, and have a marked sense of duty and discipline. Furthermore, they take pride in mastering their weapons and learning their job on the battlefield.

If the Germans are a warrior race, they are certainly militarist also. I think they love the military pageant and the panoply of war; and the feeling of strength and power that a well-organized and disciplined unit gives to each and every individual member of that unit. I am quite willing to admit that I myself share this curious attraction for the strength and elegance of beautifully trained and equipped formations, with all the art and subtlety of their movements in action against an enemy. I can well understand the enthusiasm which the soldiers—from marshals to the private soldier—showed for Napoleon; and why they followed their leader without doubt or question in his victorious campaigns. Feeling thus, they shared the glory of his conquests.

I can also understand the German soldier's high morale when Hitler seemed invincible; but I think it very remarkable that they fought their last battles just as toughly and bravely as when they were winning their first—although they must have realized that all was lost The last battles in Italy were just as bitter as any we had experienced in the Western Desert, or in the earlier stages of the Italian campaign. Like the boxer in the ring, the German soldier didn't give up until he was knocked out: and make no mistake about it, he was!

In Italy a most useful—and at times vital—role was played by an organization of which little has been heard in the war books. I refer to the Mule Corps.

Throughout the campaign the fighting, except when we reached the valley of the Po, was almost entirely over mountainous country. On the wide battle-front that stretched across the Italian peninsula from the Mediterranean to the Adriatic, a large proportion of our troops was operating in the high mountains of the Apennines, where supplies could not reach them by wheeled transport. It was necessary, therefore, to raise a Mule Corps of 30,000 animals. Italy couldn't yield anything like this number, and we had to go farther afield. Although some of the mules came from Palestine and others from Sicily and Cyprus, in the main they were gathered from countries as far away as the Argentine and Brazil. The famous horseman, Colonel Paul Rodzianko, was largely responsible for the raising of the Mule Corps, and he performed a most useful service.

A word about Intelligence—for without an efficient Intelligence organization a commander is largely blind and deaf. Mine, I would record, was first class. It dispersed the 'fog of war', and the enemy's strength and dispositions were always clearly presented to me.

To the uninformed, military intelligence in wartime is gleaned by spies and secret agents, operating in disguise behind the enemy lines. No doubt a good spy may be able to get hold of valuable information, but the difficulty is to get the information back in time for it to be of use. In the Western Desert the Long Range Desert Group wirelessed back useful information about German troop movements; in Italy the agent produced no information of any importance.

Military intelligence is not, in fact, the spectacular service of the common imagining, but a much more prosaic affair, dependent on an efficient machinery for collecting and evaluating every sort of item of information—machinery that extends from the front-line right back to Supreme Headquarters. When the mass of information has been collected, the art is to sift the wheat from the chaff, and then to lay before the commander a short clear statement.

Then there are the administrative services. My administrative staff was headed by General Sir Brian Robertson, whose experience in this vitally important field went back to the early days of the war in North Africa. In Italy, the blocked and mined ports, the demolished roads and bridges, the railway lines torn up by special machines were all additional obstacles to our advance; and the Germans continued to grow more efficient at this work of destruction as they gained more experience.

Even so, operations were never seriously altered or delayed because of any weakness in our administrative services. Full credit must be given to General Robertson and his staff for the faultless working of the machine. Through battle, flood, fire, tempest, over land and sea, they brought us all the way from Cairo via Tunis to Triest—a total distance of well over 3,000 miles—at an average speed of four miles a day. Not bad going!

What will be the verdict of history on the campaign in Italy? Although in the view of the Combined Chiefs of Staff this theatre was a secondary front, the Germans appeared to give it a rather higher rating: quite certainly they never let up in their exertions to hold on to their positions. Even so, one has to face the question: 'In the light of our war strategy, was the Italian campaign worth the effort and sacrifice it entailed?'

Let us consider the situation that existed in the summer of 1943. All Axis forces had been cleared from North Africa and by the conquest of Sicily we had opened the Mediterranean to our shipping. We were now in a position to strike against any part of Hitler's southern-held Europe and to bring his forces to battle. We enjoyed command of the sea and the air; and we had a great number of first-class fighting formations who had proved themselves on the battlefield and conquered the Afrika Korps and its Italian allies.

Of course, we could have sat down in comfortable billets in Sicily and North Africa and awaited the Normandy invasion, still nearly a year ahead. But battles are not won by inactivity—nor are wars. It is inconceivable that the flower of the British and the American armies, together with our French and Polish allies, should have

remained quiescent, leaving the Russians to do all the fighting until
'Overlord'. For although we were called upon to contribute many
of our best divisions to the Normandy operation, we were still left
with a battle-hardened fighting force of great strength which would
have withered away without action.

Thus I have no doubt at all that the launching of the Italian
campaign and its pursuance was a wise strategic decision. It forced
Hitler to fight on three fronts—and had he not promised himself
that he would never fall into the error of his predecessors by
fighting on even two? It was the Germans, not the Allies, who were
contained in Italy; and, as the record shows, the drain on their
strength was greater than the drain on our own.

Nor should it be forgotten that when the Axis forces collapsed in
May 1945, the German surrender in Italy was the first of the two
great mass surrenders in the West.

Soon after the German surrender I was told by Field-Marshal Sir
Alan Brooke that he intended to retire as Chief of the Imperial
General Staff and that I was to succeed him. Such a post was one
not to be lightly turned aside, even if I did feel that we senior
wartime commanders should step down and hand over responsibility to younger men and so not block promotion.

It was as C.I.G.S.-designate that I went to the Potsdam Conference in July 1945. During that period in Berlin I used to go to
the Prime Minister's villa in the evening to discuss the events of
the day. It was on one of these occasions that Winston Churchill
said to me: 'Let's take a stroll in the garden—there's something
very important I want to talk to you about.' I was, of course, interested and intrigued. My former confidential talks with the
Prime Minister had always been about military operations, and I
wondered what new military adventure might be in contemplation.
He said, bluntly: 'Canada has asked for you to be its next Governor-
General. I know that Brookie wants you to succeed him as
C.I.G.S., but this is a much more important post, and I hope you
will accept it.'

This was quite unexpected but not unwelcome news. Although
I had never been to Canada, my family have had close ties with the
country for several generations, and I shall never forget the splendid Canadian soldiers who played such an important part in the
Italian campaign. I agreed at once to accept the honour, with the

result that my family and I spent six of the happiest of all our years among those fine people.

But even then I was not finished with the war. One of my major tasks during the early stages of my tenure of the post was to write my despatches on the North American and Italian campaigns. I had the whole-time assistance of a staff officer who was sent to Canada by the War Office, but all the same the job took the best part of a year.

During the war no historical section of the General Staff was provided or allowed for—a great mistake. At the end of a campaign, which may last a year or much more, the C.-in-C. is expected to write up his official despatch from a mass of material which takes even an expert considerable time to sort out. Officially no officer was allowed to keep a personal diary, although we know today that this rule was broken. The Americans were wiser; for members of the United States Army historical section accompanied their troops in action.

One final reminiscence of Winston Churchill is precious to me.

After the General Election of 1945, when our great war leader was turned out of office by the people's vote, I perceived an opportunity to repay in some small measure something of the debt I owed him for the trust, friendship, and support that he had always extended to me throughout the war years. As a small gesture to show my affection for him I made this suggestion in a letter: 'If you would like it, I will requisition a villa for you on the shores of Lake Como. I will make all the arrangements as regards a domestic staff and supplies of food and wine, and I will arrange for a guard from your own regiment, the 4th Hussars, to safeguard your privacy and person.' He was able to accept the invitation, and spent a month at the villa.

I purposely avoided interfering with his holiday, though I did stay with him for just one week-end, when we spent the Sunday painting. At one point he turned to me and said: 'You know, when I was turned out of office, I felt it to be a very hard thing after all I had done.' Then with a smile, and waving his hand towards the scene he was painting, he added: 'But life has its compensations, you know—if I was still in office I wouldn't be here to enjoy this lovely climate and marvellous landscape.'

BATTLE MAPS

Italy

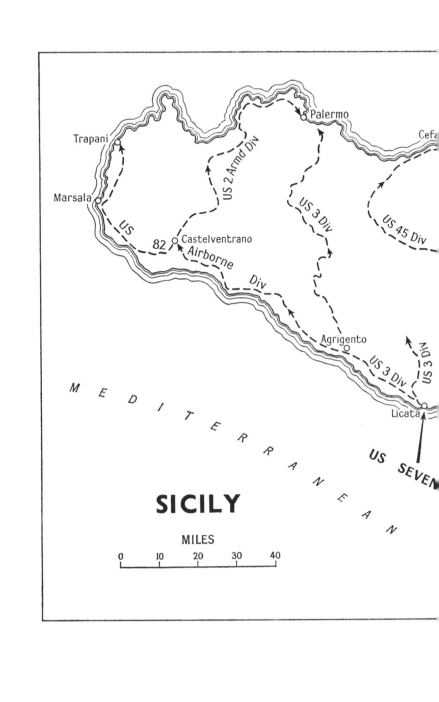

Trapani

Marsala

US

82

Castelventrano

Airborne

Div

US 2 Armd Div

Palermo

Cefa

US 3 Div

US 45 Div

Agrigento

US 3 Div

US 3 Div

Licata

M E D I T E R R A N E A N

US SEVEN

SICILY

MILES

0   10   20   30   40

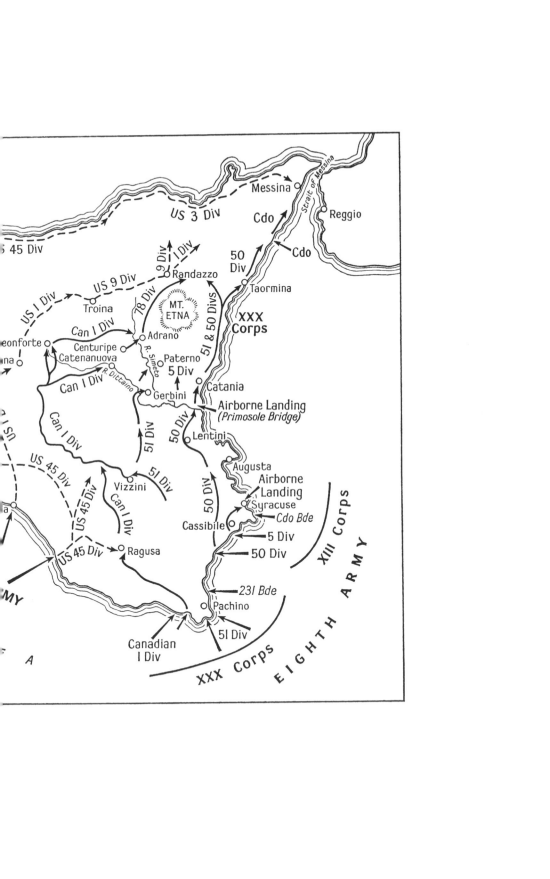

Italy

A NECESSARY preliminary to the invasion of Sicily was the capture of Pantelleria. The island, lying a hundred miles due east of Tunis, served the enemy as an advanced observation post and a fighter base. Only through the mouth of the island's one tiny harbour along its rocky coast-line was it possible to land troops from assault boats. On 11 June 1943, after six days of air bombardment, the Italians discreetly emerged from their cavernous shelters to surrender as the British troops landed. The invasion of Sicily was to follow in the small hours of 10 July, in accordance with a decision of the Combined Chiefs of Staff taken away back in January, that it should be launched during 'the favourable period of the July moon'. Thus, on 9 July, a great armada assembled east and west of Malta. A rising gale abated only as the leading craft closed the island.

SICILY

Eighth Army provided the British contribution to the ground forces. It was to land on the east coast of the island and advance northward on Messina. En route it would be confronted by Mount Etna. United States Seventh Army, under Patton, would disembark on the south coast and cover the flank of Eighth Army. The concentration of these forces was in itself a feat of some magnitude. Canadian 1 Division sailed from the United Kingdom; the Americans had brought a division direct from the United States; other divisions embarked from African, Egyptian, and Palestinian ports. On the other hand, the Germans could easily pour in reinforcements from the Italian mainland across the Strait of Messina—only two miles wide and well protected by coastal batteries and anti-aircraft guns.

The airborne invasion that preceded the landings from the sea caught the full fury of the storm. United States 82 Airborne Division was scattered in considerable confusion over the hinterland of Gela, and British 1 Airborne Division lost a large proportion of its glider force on the passage from Africa; but a sufficient number landed south of Syracuse to prevent the destruction of the port's river and rail bridges. Of a glider force of seventy-three officers and men, four officers and fifteen men survived till mid-afternoon, when they were relieved by seaborne patrols. South of Syracuse a commando brigade and 5 and 50 British Divisions of XIII Corps secured their beachhead, and 5 Division entered the town. Canadian 1 and British 51 Divisions secured the Pachino peninsula and its airstrip. The first day closed with the capture of Gela by United States 1 and 45 Divisions; and United States 3 Division established a beachhead round Licata and secured the airfields behind the town.

Next morning the battle for Sicily opened in earnest with a counter-attack by German armour towards Gela; it was repelled only with the assistance of naval gunfire. Nevertheless the American right flank succeeded in establishing contact with the Canadians of XXX Corps near Ragusa. Again it was naval gunfire, in face of German armour, that assisted British XIII Corps to capture Augusta; while British XXX Corps continued its advance north-westward on distant Enna and Leonforte. On the night of the 13th XIII Corps attacked south of Catania; but the vital airfield in its neighbourhood resisted capture. On this same night 1 Parachute Brigade attempted the capture of the 400-feet long Primosole bridge across the Simeto—the sole exit from the southern hills into the Catania plain: where, incidentally, the Hermann Göring Panzer Division had already almost completed its concentration. The battle for the bridge—a battle of all arms, with German paratroops in action—was fought through four days; and it was not until the 17th that 50 Division was able to establish a bridgehead. On XXX Corps axis of advance, Vizzini had been taken on the 14th: whereupon the Canadians took the lead and drove towards Leonforte.

By this time United States Seventh Army, in accordance with my directive, was developing its thrust northward on the left of Eighth Army, in order to cut off enemy forces in the west of the island; and United States 1 Division entered Enna as the Canadians reached Leonforte. To the west Agrigento was captured; and United States 3 and 82 Airborne Divisions, now reinforced by United States 2 Armoured Division, were able to continue their advance.

Meantime Eighth Army was definitely held on the Catania plain; and after 51 Highland Division had been finally checked at Gerbini there was no alternative but to thrust forward Eighth Army's left round Mount Etna. To assist this new effort I summoned 78 Division—formerly of First Army—from Africa. United States Seventh

Ortona

●ROME

R. Sangro

R. Trigno

Campobasso

Cassino

Vinchiaturo

US V
Cor

R. Volturno

X Corps   Caserta

Naples

TYRRHENIAN   SEA

US
FIFTH
ARMY

Salern

X Corps

US VI Corps

SOUTHERN ITALY
To end of Oct 1943

MILES

50   0   50   100

SICIL

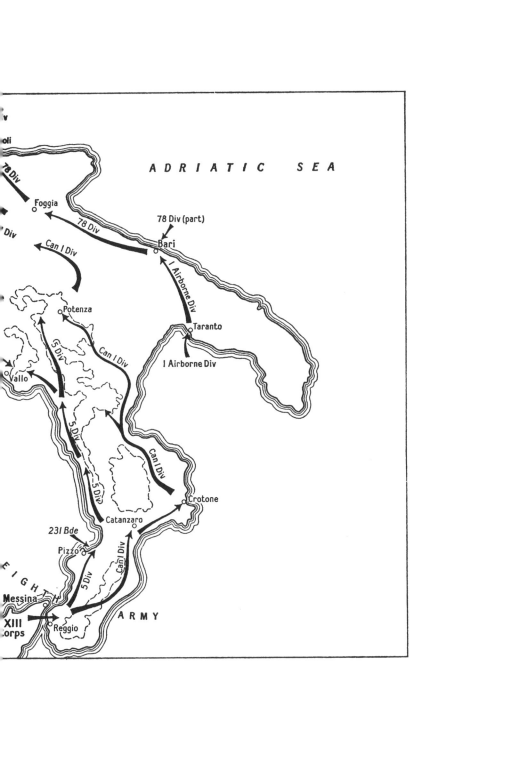

ADRIATIC SEA

78 Div

oli

78 Div

Div

78 Div (part)

Foggia

78 Div

Bari

Can I Div

I Airborne Div

Potenza

Taranto

Can I Div

I Airborne Div

Vallo

5 Div

Can I Div

5 Div

5 Div

Can I Div

Crotone

Catanzaro

231 Bde

Pizzo

5 Div

Can I Div

EIGH

Messina

XIII
orps

Reggio

ARMY

Army had been more fortunate in its own advance. On 22 July Palermo surrendered to United States 2 Armoured and 3 Divisions without resistance; and by the following day, with the capture of Marsala and Trapani, all fighting had ceased in the western corner of the island. I now ordered Patton to advance on Messina with his left on the coast.

The regrouping of the armies took time, and it was not possible to start the final phase of the campaign before the end of July. German resistance was still desperate in all sectors: on the south-western side of Etna; between Catenanuova and Centuripe, where the newly arrived 78 Division was operating; and at Troina, under attack by United States 1 Division; and along the coast towards Messina, despite the assistance rendered to United States 3 Division by landings from the sea.

On 7 August, 78 Division at last entered Adrano, key to the Etna defences, and the enemy's withdrawal now became general. On the Catania front, 50 Division was now advancing up the coast road, after a fierce rearguard action on the edge of the town. On 13 August, United States 9 Division captured Randazzo and met 78 Division, approaching south of the town. On the coastal side the enemy had now broken contact with 50 and 51 Divisions—50 occupying Taormina on the 15th.

The landing farther north of a tank squadron and a commando was too late to cut off the enemy rearguard, but part of the force joined United States 3 Division in Messina on the 17th—the day following the American entry. The conquest of Sicily was complete; but the only surrenders were Italian. The Germans, through their skill in demolitions and last-hour resistance, had made good their retreat across the Strait of Messina to the mainland.

SOUTHERN ITALY
to end of October 1943

The invasion of the mainland of Europe was opened by Eighth Army. Under cover of a heavy bombardment provided by all three services, the leading divisions began to cross the Strait of Messina in the early hours of 3 September 1943. Landing at Reggio, Canadian 1 and British 5 Divisions of XIII Corps encountered no resistance. 5 Division advanced up the 'toe'; the Canadians along the eastern coast road. The country generally lent itself to delaying action by small units co-ordinated with skilfully sited demolitions. On 5 September, 5 Division clashed with German rearguards; but, with the entry into Catanzaro on 10 September, the invasion force was established from sea to sea.

Now the immediate mission of Eighth Army was to maintain pressure to relieve the main Allied invasion front on the Tyrthenian shore, with Naples as the objective. To assist these landings in the Gulf of Salerno, part of British 1 Airborne Division was put ashore at Taranto, unopposed, on 9 September; 231 Malta Brigade— veterans of the siege of Malta—together with a commando, had landed at Pizzo a day earlier. Montgomery, still commanding Eighth Army, comments on his Army's mission: 'We marched and fought 300 miles in 17 days, against an enemy whose use of demolitions caused us bridging problems of the first magnitude. The hairpin bends on the roads were such that any distance measured on the map as, say, 10 miles was 20 miles on the ground.' Here would appear to be an opportunity to pay a tribute to a distinguished British invention. Whatever the valour of the fighting troops, without the 'Bailey' to bridge the rivers and ravines of Italy, the campaign would have been abortive from the outset.

SALERNO

The Allied landings in the Gulf of Salerno went in on the morning of 9 September. To the north, British X Corps, under command of United States Fifth Army, landed 46 and 56 Divisions, with two commandos and three battalions of United States Rangers on the western flank. Despite the enemy's artillery fire, Maiori and Vietri, and Salerno itself, were speedily entered: behind them lay the mountain passes that led, past Vesuvius, into the plain of Naples. On the right, 56 Division, greatly assisted by naval gunfire, progressed against stiffening opposition to secure the Montecorvino airfield; but Battapaglia—a road and railway junction—resisted capture.

United States VI Corps of Fifth Army landed south of the River Sele. Its 36 Division, untried in battle, had difficulty in establishing a beachhead; but from the northern American beaches the advance went forward to the day's objectives, and, to the south, by darkness the infantry had established forward positions on the nose of Monte Soprano, about five miles inland east of Paestum. United States 45 Division landed the next day; and, at a time when the enemy was moving strong forces northward to concentrate against the British, the two United States divisions were able to consolidate and extend their gains. But contact had not been established between the Allied formations.

Meanwhile 56 Division was engaged in a bitter struggle for Battapaglia: it was won and lost again. On 11 September, the division fought hard to capture Mount Eboli. Steep-sided and fifteen hundred feet high, it dominated most of 56 Division's area. But gains

169

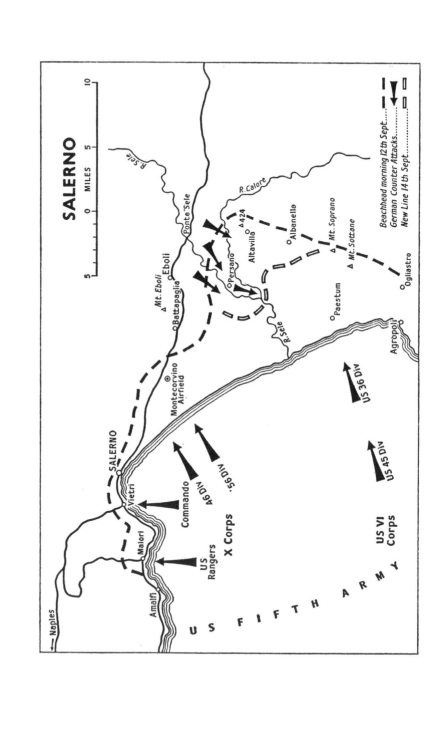

SALERNO

MILES

Naples

Amalfi

Maiori

Vietri

SALERNO

US Rangers

Commando

46 DIV

56 DIV

X Corps

Montecorvino
Airfield

US 36 Div

US 45 Div

US VI
Corps

Agropoli

Paestum

R. Sele

Ogliastro

△ Mt. Sottane

△ Mt. Soprano

Albanella

Altavilla

△ 424

Persano

Battapaglia

Eboli

△ Mt. Eboli

Ponte Sele

R. Sele

R. Calore

US F I F T H A R M Y

Beachhead morning 12th Sept......

German Counter Attacks...........

New Line 14 th Sept..............

were small; once more Battapaglia was won and lost—the withdrawal, on this occasion, necessitating a shortening of the British line. Moreover, on 12 and 13 September, German armoured forces from the north moved in to attack, in testing strength, X Corps' mountain positions behind Malori and Vietri.

The Germans were also disputing the advance of the American left, and on the morning of 12 September had unleashed a strong attack down both banks of the Sele. The Americans were driven from Persano, Hill 424, and the villages of Altavilla and Albanella. This enemy thrust threatened to reach the sea and cut the Allied forces in two. American artillery, aided by naval gunfire and air strikes, averted disaster, and enabled United States VI Corps to form a firm defensive line. A few days later, on 16 September, on the extreme right flank, VI Corps made contact with patrols of Eighth Army; and a general German withdrawal gamed momentum. On this same day, on Eighth Army front, the Canadians made contact with advanced troops from Taranto; three days later they were in Potenza.

Although, in the Salerno sector, the Germans had withdrawn quickly in front of the Americans, they challenged fiercely the advance of British X Corps through the mountains on the road to Naples; and on 23 September the corps was compelled to lay on a formal attack: 7 Armoured Division had now arrived on the scene, and it went in with 46 Division, 56 Division operating on the right flank of the attack. The main battle lasted through three days. Thereafter, in pouring rain, German rearguards still resisted stoutly; and the King's Dragoon Guards were not to enter Naples till 1 October. Meanwhile Eighth Army—now reinforced by the landing of part of 78 Division and 4 Armoured Brigade at Ban on 23 September—had advanced to the key airfields of Foggia—vacated by the enemy on 27 September.

My orders to Fifteenth Army Group at this time were still to press on, with Rome as the ultimate objective. Thus 78 Division pushed along the coast while Canadian 1 Division advanced through the mountains. By 3 October, with the assistance of a commando landed beyond the town, 78 Division had secured the port of Termoli. After the arrival of reinforcements the Germans counter-attacked and re-entered the town; but four days later the situation had been restored, with the assistance of another brigade of 78 Division. The enemy now fell back to a line covering the Trigno; but XIII Corps was compelled to pause for supply—although the Canadians continued their steady advance through the mountains despite considerable opposition. By 11 October the Corps line ran Termoli-Vinchiaturo.

ADRIATIC

SEA

Pescara

Ortona

R. Sangro

HIGHWAY 5

W I N T E R   L I N E

E I G H T H   A R M Y

ROME

HIGHWAY 6

Cisterna

Anzio

HIGHWAY 7

R. Liri

Cassino

Venafro

Mignano

F I F T H   A R M Y

Caserta

TYRRHENIAN

SEA

R. Garigliano

R. Volturno

THE WINTER LINE
END OF 1943

MILES

10   0   10   20   30   40

United States Fifth Army was now thrusting forward to the Volturno—a difficult obstacle both to British X Corps on the Tyrrhenian side and to United States VI Corps, which had come up through the mountains on the right. The struggle for the crossings began in the now usual rain on the night of 12 October, with British 46 and 56 Divisions on the left and United States VI Corps farther inland. The struggle lasted through several days. When the crossings were achieved, United States Fifth Army resumed its march through the mountains and along the coast. On 23 October, Eighth Army, too, resumed operations, faced with a similar task—that of breaking the Trigno river line. In the rain and the mud, little more could be accomplished than the establishment of minor bridgeheads. As in an earlier war, *la boue* was becoming an even more formidable enemy than the Boche. Moreover, it was now becoming evident that the Germans were bringing down strong reinforcements from the north; and the Allied armies were shortly to be confronted by a formidable belt of mountain fortifications.

THE WINTER LINE
end of 1943

The fortifications now facing the Allied armies, known to the Germans as the Gustav Line and to the Allied soldiers as the Winter Line, stretched from behind the River Garigliano to Ortona on the Adriatic Sea. It covered the two main routes to Rome from the south-Highway 7, near the coast, and Highway 6, which enters the Liri Valley at Cassino.

At the end of October, United States Fifth Army, with British X Corps still under command, began to advance through the mountains from the Volturno bridgeheads to close up to the Winter Line, in rain, and cold, and snow. On the left, X Corps began to approach the Garigliano on 2 November. United States VI Corps had a rougher passage before securing Mignano and Venafro: the Germans had sited their own Winterstellung in front of Mignano and above Venafro. X Corps then attacked, with limited success, the mountain mass that dominates Highway 6 to the south of Mignano. The Americans made equally little progress in their advance towards that name of destiny, Cassino. By mid-November a standstill had been ordered in Fifth Army for regrouping.

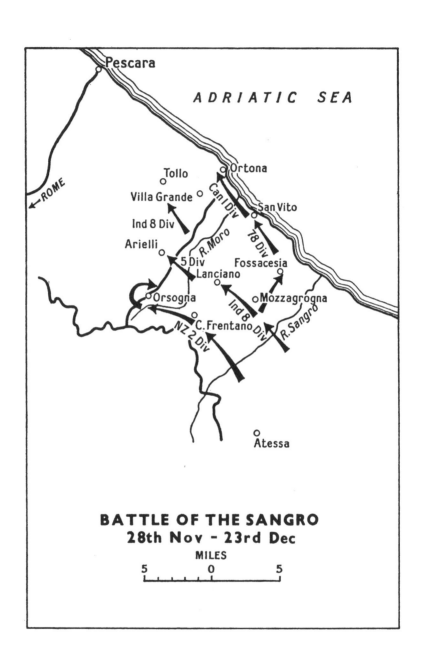

ADRIATIC SEA

Pescara

← ROME

Tollo

Villa Grande

Ortona

Can I Div

San Vito

Ind 8 Div

78 Div

Arielli

R. Moro

5 Div

Fossacesia

Lanciano

Orsogna

Ind 8 Div

Mozzagrogna

C. Frentano

NZ 2 Div

R. Sangro

Atessa

BATTLE OF THE SANGRO
28th Nov - 23rd Dec

MILES

5   0   5

BATTLE OF THE SANGRO
28 November–23 December 1943

Eighth Army resumed its operations at the beginning of November, when V Corps (5, 78 and Indian 8 Divisions) advanced across the Trigno. By the 8th, the leading divisions were overlooking the considerable obstacle of the Sangro river, where the enemy defences formed part of the eastern end of the Winter Line. Heavy rain delayed the continuance of operations, but a firm foothold was obtained beyond the Sangro before the main attack went in on 28 November. Indian 8 Division made progress before being checked by counter-attack. On the left, New Zealand 2 Division was coming forward; and by the night of the 29th it could be said that V Corps had broken into the Winter Line.

Next day 1 Armoured Brigade took Fossacesia and the Indian Division resumed its offensive. Although the Germans had again been strongly reinforced, by 4 December, Canadian 1 Division, replacing 78 Division, was past San Vito; Indian 8 Division had captured Lanciano; the New Zealanders had advanced beyond Castel Frentano and were now threatening Orsogna; and the Canadians were pushing on toward Ortona, with naval gunfire and the Desert Air Force assisting their advance. Nevertheless Ortona was only to fall after a full week's fighting. Farther inland, Indian 8 Division, making for Tollo, captured Villa Grande, and the newly brought in 5 Division took Arielli. On the left flank, the New Zealanders, though not in Orsogna, had reached the high ground north-east of the town. But weather conditions, with no promise of improvement, made fighting conditions for the troops intolerable, and at Christmas, with my approval, Montgomery brought operations to a close.

CASSINO
January–February 1944

United States Fifth Army, with not less gallantry, had resumed its offensive at the beginning of the month. On 1 December, British X Corps began another attack upon the southern end of the mountain mass south-west of Mignano. This attack, by British 46 and 56 Divisions, was successful; and the recently formed United States II Corps on their right was also able to advance and to attack on either side of Highway 6 and make considerable progress. Farther north, United States VI Corps fought forward in the mountains north-east of Cassino, with part of the French Expeditionary Corps, newly arrived from Africa, on its flank. But necessary regrouping brought operations to a halt by mid-December.

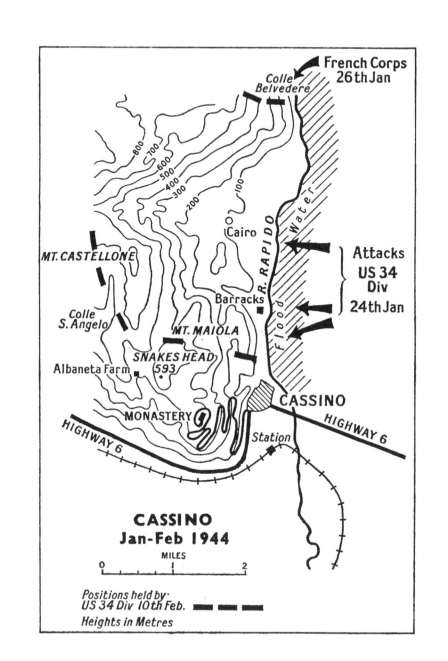

French Corps
26th Jan

Colle
Belvedere

800
700
600
500
400
300
200
100

MT. CASTELLONE

Cairo

R. RAPIDO

Water

Attacks
US 34
Div
24th Jan

Colle
S. Angelo

Barracks

Flood

MT. MAIOLA

SNAKES HEAD
593

Albaneta Farm

MONASTERY

CASSINO

HIGHWAY 6

Station

HIGHWAY 6

**CASSINO
Jan-Feb 1944**

MILES

0   1   2

Positions held by
US 34 Div 10th Feb.

Heights in Metres

Before they were re-opened various changes in command were to take place. Eisenhower, C.-in-C. Allied Force, left the Mediterranean for the 'Overlord' command in Europe. He was succeeded by General (now Field-Marshal Lord) Wilson, then C.-in-C., Middle East. In March 1944, his title was changed to Supreme Allied Commander, Mediterranean. Montgomery took farewell of Eighth Army for the command of the Twenty-First Army Group, which was to open the Second Front in north-west Europe. He was succeeded by Lieutenant-General Sir Oliver Leese. My own command had now taken on the title of the Allied Armies in Italy.

ANZIO
22–23 January 1944

The seaborne landings at Anzio were conceived as an alternative to forcing the Winter Line by frontal attack. The port lies only thirty miles south of Rome and more than seventy miles behind the right flank of the line. A bold thrust from the Anzio beaches was calculated to cut the main routes to the city, Highways 6 and 7, and thereby sever the main communications of the Germans to the south. The plain of Anzio stretches inland for some twenty miles to the Alban Hills, which rise abruptly in volcanic slopes to a height of some three thousand feet.

Thus on 22 January 1944, in fine weather, United States VI Corps, comprising United States 3 and British 1 Divisions, landed unopposed at Nettuno and Anzio from a fleet of 243 vessels—Dutch, Greek, Polish, and French, as well as British and American. The beachhead extended from the Mussolini Canal to the River Moletta.

The landings had been designed as the climax to an offensive due to be launched on the main front on 17 January, and were intended to lead directly to the capture of Rome. With this end in view, a United States Fifth Army Field Order of 12 January had ordered the corps commander to secure his beachhead and then advance to the Alban Hills. Shortly after midday on the 22nd, there was a continuous perimeter round the land area and both the American and British troops were firmly established; the following day was employed in consolidating an area approximately seven miles deep by fifteen miles wide within a perimeter of some twenty-six miles, and heavy guns, tanks, ammunition, and stores were disembarked. No advance was ordered.

In order to keep the enemy fully occupied Fifth Army renewed its pressure on the main front-always with some hope of a decisive success. On 17 January, British X Corps on the left forced the passage of the Garigliano but failed, after prolonged efforts, to

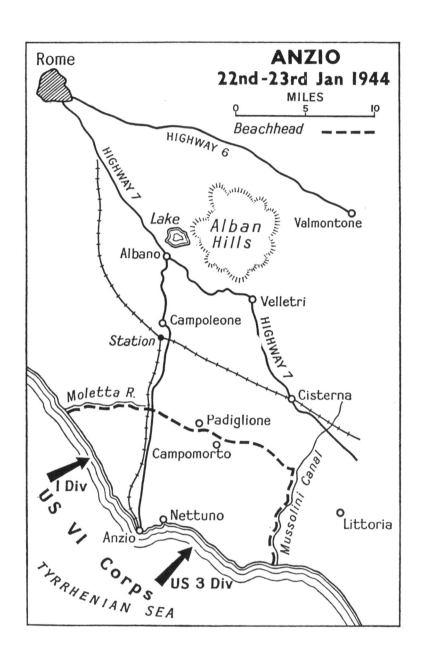

ANZIO
22nd-23rd Jan 1944

MILES

Beachhead ----

Rome

HIGHWAY 6

HIGHWAY 7

Valmontone

Lake

Alban Hills

Albano

Velletri

Campoleone

HIGHWAY 7

Station

Moletta R.

Cisterna

Padiglione

Campomorto

I Div

US VI Corps

Mussolini Canal

Littoria

Nettuno

Anzio

US 3 Div

TYRRHENIAN SEA

make sufficient headway by undertaking a turning movement inland. On 20 January, United States 36 Division—now with United States II Corps—attempted the crossing of the Rapido about five miles south of Cassino. The attack failed, with heavy loss. North of Cassino, the French Corps made progress into the mountains, but without penetrating the enemy's main defensive system.

On 24 January, United States 36 Division again attacked across the swollen upper Rapido north of Cassino town and made painful progress west and south-west among the mountains. Finally, in mid-February, the American left arrived on the threshold of Cassino and clung to positions not far from the northern side of Monastery Hill. Beyond the hill a succession of crags and peaks extends west and north-west, overlooking the Liri Valley and Highway 6. Away to the north the French were still engaged in desultory mountain warfare.

Meanwhile at Anzio the German forces were building up: Hitler had ordered the elimination of what he described as the 'abscess' south of Rome; and when United States VI Corps, now reinforced by two American divisions—1 Armoured and 45 Infantry—attacked toward Cisterna and Campoleone on 29 January, it could gain only a narrow salient, with its peak at Campoleone station. On 3 February, German counter-attacks obliterated the salient. For the rest of the month attack and counter-attack followed in quick succession; not until early March was the enemy effort exhausted. But it had resulted in absorbing a considerable proportion of the Allied strength. On the British side, 5 and 56 Divisions had been brought in; on the American side, United States 34 Division and a Special Service Force.

CASSINO
15–24 March 1944

To assist Fifth Army to maintain pressure on its front during the critical weeks at Anzio, early in February two divisions were drawn from Eighth Army—New Zealand 2 and Indian 4—to form New Zealand II Corps. The task of the corps was to take Cassino and break through into the Liri Valley. Before the middle of the month it had relieved the Americans in the Cassino sector—the Indians taking over the precarious Allied positions north of Monastery Hill.

The first Indian 4 Division attack went in on the night of x6 February, after the air bombardment of the abbey on Monastery Hill by a mixed fleet of 255 heavy and medium bombers. Such was the nature of the ground that only a few troops could be deployed; and this attack, and another on the following night, achieved little. After darkness on the 17th, the division attacked in greater strength

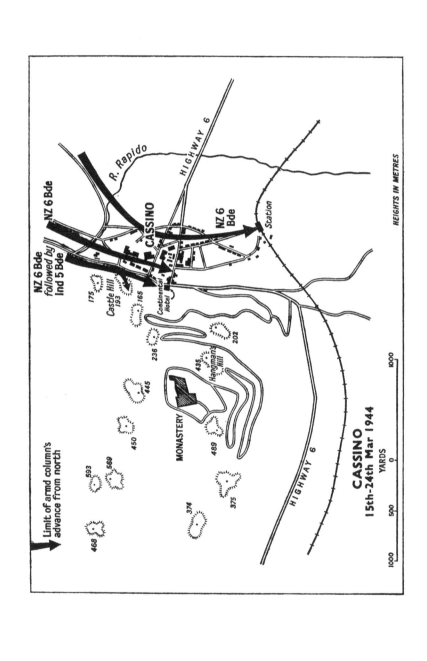

Limit of armd column's
advance from north

NZ 6 Bde
followed by
Ind 5 Bde

NZ 6 Bde

R. Rapido

HIGHWAY 6

CASSINO

NZ 6
Bde

Station

175

Castle Hill
193

165

Continental
Hotel

236

202

445

435
Hangman's
Hill

MONASTERY

450

489

593

569

374

375

468

HIGHWAY 6

CASSINO
15th-24th Mar 1944

YARDS

1000   500   0   1000

HEIGHTS IN METRES

from the north, while a New Zealand brigade advanced on Cassino town from the south-east. An Indian brigade, after a bitter struggle, reached Points 593 and 450, north-west of Monastery Hill. Thereafter they could do no more than repulse a succession of determined counter-attacks. The Maori battalion of the New Zealand Division crossed the flooded Rapido in assault boats and advanced through swamps and minefields under heavy fire from the town and from Monastery Hill. Later in the day, after reaching the railway station, the Maoris were attacked by tanks and infantry. Since it had proved impossible to reinforce them they were withdrawn across the Rapido.

Because of the atrocious weather nearly a month was to elapse before the New Zealand Corps could return to the attack. On 15 March, after an all-obliterating air bombardment of Cassino town, the corps put in an infantry assault. A New Zealand brigade led the way into the shattered town by the roads from the north, then turning west to take Castle Hill. Some progress was made towards Highway 6; but the defence, assisted by rain and darkness, was as stubborn as ever. An Indian brigade now took over Castle Hill and captured Point 165. Point 236 eluded capture, but a solitary company went through to establish itself on Hangman's Hill—the nearest approach yet to the ruins of the abbey on Monastery Hill. Appropriately enough, thereafter it could do no more than hang on—every attack inviting a counter-attack.

Armour could be only of limited assistance to the New Zealanders on their southward advance through the rubble of Cassino town; and although, like the Maoris before them, they reached the railway station, on 16 March—and, on the 18th, Point 202—the Germans continued to cling desperately to its western side. A New Zealand armoured column coming down from the north was checked near Point 593 with the loss of many of its tanks; and despite sustained intensity of effort the New Zealanders failed to secure the Continental Hotel—now a battleground—and control of Highway 6, and on 22 March had to be content with stabilizing their position on a line running from Castle Hill to the railway station. The troops on Hangman's Hill and Point 202 were thus isolated. Two nights later they were withdrawn. The aching struggle for an entry into the Liri Valley—and for Monastery Hill—was not to reopen until 11 May.

CASSINO–LIRI VALLEY
11–29 May 1944

Eighth Army now took over the task of opening the Liri Valley—the path to Rome. On II May, XIII Corps attacked across the Rapido, south of Cassino, with British 4 and Indian 8 Divisions.

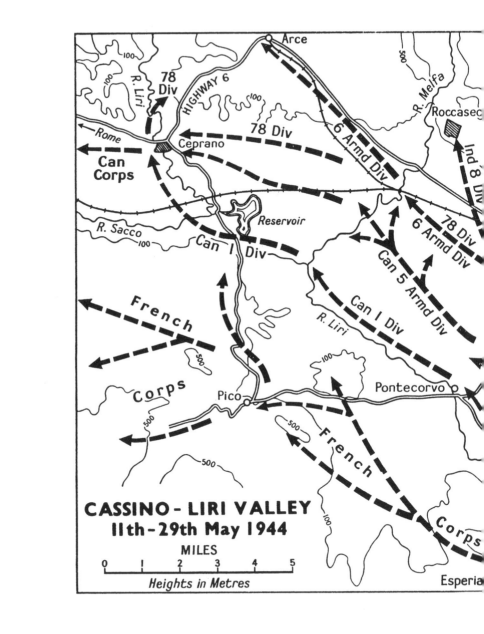

Arce

78
Div

HIGHWAY 6

R. Liri

100

100

500

R. Melfa

Roccasec

Ind 8 Div

78 Div

6 Armd Div

Rome

Can
Corps

Ceprano

78 Div
6 Armd Div

R. Sacco

100

Reservoir

Can I Div

Can 5 Armd Div

French

R. Liri

Can I Div

500

Corps

Pico

100

Pontecorvo

500

French

500

500

100

Corps

CASSINO - LIRI VALLEY
11th - 29th May 1944

MILES

0   1   2   3   4   5

Heights in Metres

Esperia

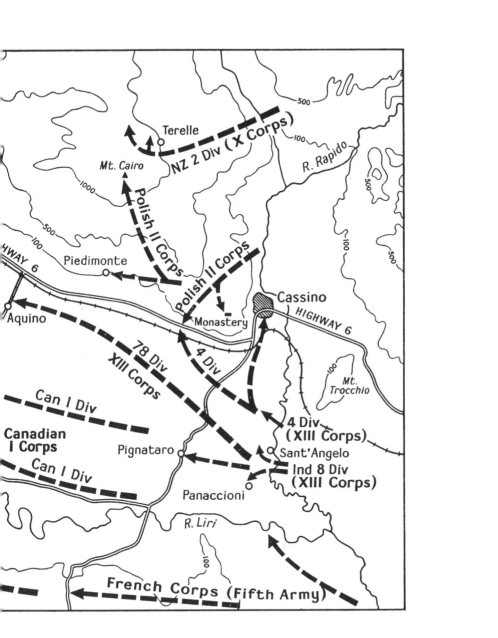

After three days of hard fighting, bridgeheads were established north and south of Sant' Angelo and the village was occupied; Indian troops secured the hamlet of Panaccioni on the southern flank. Meanwhile Polish II Corps had attacked Cassino from the north— but still without avail. On the left of Eighth Army, the French Corps tackled the Aurunci mountains to the south and made good progress toward Pico. In the coastal sector, United States II Corps—85 and 88 Divisions—advanced from the Garigliano bridgehead, maintaining contact with the French; but their gains at first were small and their losses heavy. On 17 May, 85 Division entered Formia.

In the Liri Valley the slow grind continued. British 4 Division reached the Pignataro road on 15 May—Indian 8 Division having captured the village itself; 78 Division, coming through the bridgehead, advanced north-westward toward Highway 6; farther to the left, Canadian 1 Division relieved the Indians—Canadian 1 Corps taking over the sector. On 17 May, Highway 6 was crossed by 4 Division, and Cassino town was at last secured. The next day, the Polish standard flew above Monastery Hill, and Polish II Corps established contact with patrols of 78 Division on Highway 6. The French, too, had met with success in their mountain advance, occupying Esperia; and, on the left, United States II Corps was in pursuit of an enemy retreating in the direction of Fondi.

When Canadian 1 Division advanced with Frosinone as the ultimate objective, the problem in the Liri Valley was one of traffic congestion; and across the valley lay another belt of fortifications— part of it following the Aquino–Pontecorvo road—known as the Hitler Line; but it had already been outflanked to the south by the French advance, and, on 23 May, the Canadians broke through between Aquino and Pontecorvo, and Pontecorvo itself was taken. The previous day the French had captured Pico; Polish II Corps, again in action, captured Piedimonte on the 25th, and, in the mountains to the north, occupied the formidable Monte Cairo.

Canadian 5 Armoured and I Divisions now pressed forward to the Melfa river and to Ceprano, occupied on the 26th; British 6 Armoured and 78 Divisions also reached the Melfa; Indian 8 Division turned north to secure Roccasecca, beyond Highway 6; British 6 Armoured Division fought hard on the road to Arce, taken on the 29th; and 78 Division passed Ceprano and turned north up the valley of the upper Liri. The Canadians were now heading for Frosinone; and, in the coastal sector of Fifth Army, United States 88 Division of II Corps had entered Fondi on 20 May. By the morning of the 24th, United States 85 Division had won the battle of Terracina. Both these towns are on the road to Anzio.

ANZIO
February–March 1944

After four months—the original landings having taken place on 22 January—the Anzio bridgehead was now to pay off. The perimeter was manned, at the last, from left to right, by British 5 and 1 Divisions, United States 45 and 34 Divisions, and an Engineer Combat Regiment; there stood in reserve United States 1 Armoured and 3 Divisions; and by 22 May the last convoy bringing United States 36 Division had arrived off Nettuno.

The next day, in a drizzle of rain, at a quarter to six in the morning, American artillery opened fire and light bombers and fighter-bombers attacked the neighbourhood of Cisterna. On 24 May, United States 1 Armoured Division crossed Highway 7, north of Cisterna. On 25 May, in the neighbourhood of Cisterna, the enemy broke. That same day United States VI Corps—from Anzio—made contact with United States II Corps—from Terracina.

General Mark Clark, Commanding General of the United States Fifth Army, issued instructions early on the 26th to launch a direct attack on Rome—although, as early as 5 May, with Mark Clark's agreement, I had decided to aim the American attack at Valmontone, in order to cut the German line of retreat along Highway 7. The change of direction of 34 and 45 Divisions of United States VI Corps was effected with remarkable speed: within twelve hours the new attack had begun. Thus the drive on Valmontone was reduced in weight when United States 3 Division, continuing its original thrust to Valmontone, met and was held by the Hermann Göring Panzer Division. Nearer the coast British 1 and 5 Divisions advanced towards the Tiber.

ADVANCE ON AND THE CAPTURE OF ROME
11 May–7 June 1944

United States II Corps and the French Corps now converged on Valmontone, where the Germans stood firm until 1 June—when the Americans, crossing Highway 6, turned for Rome. The French, on the right, also crossed the road, heading for Highway 5. Not till 3 June did the Germans, on United States II Corps front, withdraw in the direction of Albano; whereupon its I Armoured Division went through the infantry and prepared to enter Rome by the Via Appia—otherwise Highway 7. Meanwhile Eighth Army had continued to pursue the enemy on and north of Highway 6: X Corps headed north-west toward Balsorano; on XIII Corps front,

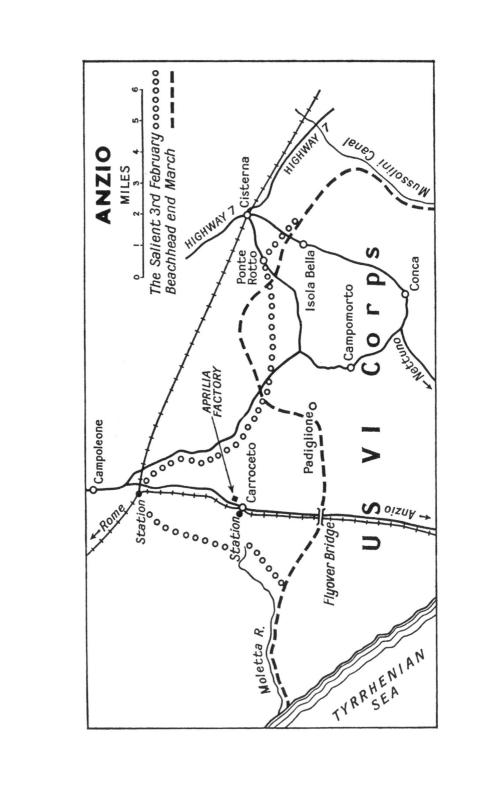

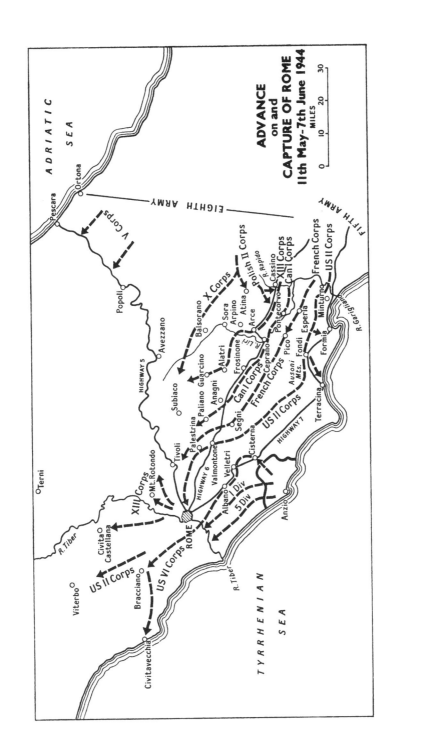

ADVANCE
on and
CAPTURE OF ROME
11th May-7th June 1944

MILES

0   10   20   30

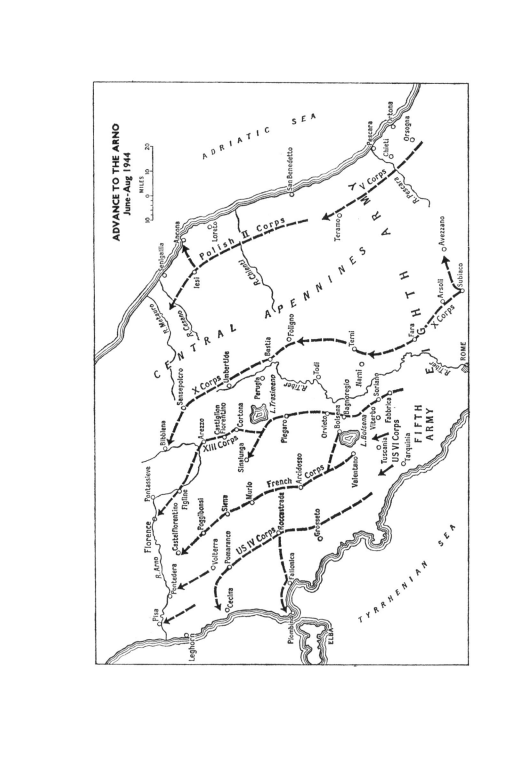

78 Division entered Alatri on 2 June, with Indian 8 Division directed on Guarcino. On the left the Canadians were through Frosinone, and still advancing.

With Valmontone clear of the enemy, United States II Corps found its advance on Rome unopposed, and battalions of 85 and 88 Divisions, in the company of an armoured column from United States VI Corps, entered the city on 4 June. East of Rome, Eighth Army turned to cut the northward retreat of the Germans across Highway 5. On the day that Rome fell, Indian 8 Division of XIII Corps had reached Guarcino, and South African 6 Armoured Division—now also of XIII Corps—was approaching Paliano.

The Allied advance did not pause with the occupation of Rome. On the Adriatic side a German withdrawal enabled British V Corps to reach Highway 5, between Pescara and Popoli; X Corps, headed by New Zealand 2 Division, took the road from Sora to Avezzano; and Indian 8 Division—now under X Corps—led the way to Subiaco. XIII Corps moved westward and advanced astride the Tiber. Fast of the river, 6 Armoured Division had brisk engagements at and near Monte Rotondo on 7 and 8 June; on the western side, South African 6 Armoured Division went ahead and captured Civita Castellana. On the Fifth Army front, United States VI Corps—which had now released British 1 and 5 Divisions—led the advance from Rome. Apart from a sharp skirmish at Bracciano on 6 June, little opposition was encountered, and the port of Civitavecchia was secured without fighting that same night.

ADVANCE TO THE ARNO
June–August 1944

On 7 June, I ordered an advance to the Arno with all possible speed—with the object of reaching the northern Apennines before the enemy could organize his defences among the mountains. The main advance of the Fifth and Eighth Armies would be west of the central Apennines, with some minor activity on the Adriatic side.

On British X Corps front, Indian 8 Division was in Arsoli on 9 June and New Zealand 2 Division reached Avezzano the next day; but the corps, much impeded by demolitions and difficult hill country, did not reach Terni until the 15th. British 6 Armoured Division—transferred from XIII Corps—then passed through Todi and pressed on toward Perugia, while Indian 8 Division captured Foligno. The advance on Perugia was made astride the Tiber, and the Indians were sharply engaged in the neighbourhood of Bastia; but, with the abandonment of Perugia by the Germans on 20 June, the pursuit to the north was resumed.

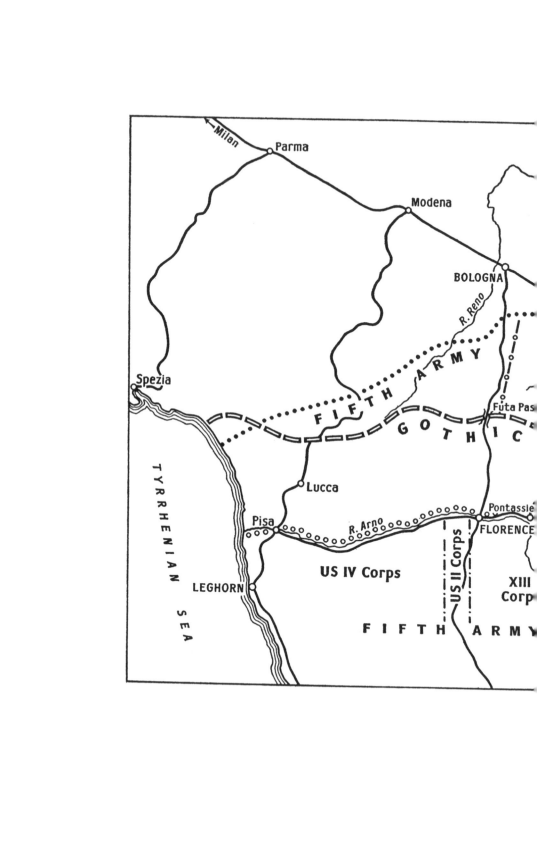

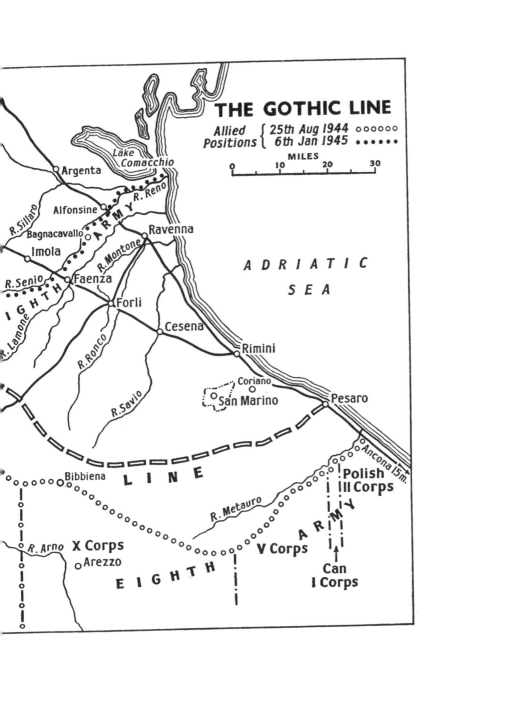

THE GOTHIC LINE

Allied Positions { 25th Aug 1944 ○○○○○
6th Jan 1945 ••••••

MILES

0   10   20   30

Lake Comacchio

Argenta

Alfonsine

R.Sillaro

Bagnacavallo

Imola

R.Senio

R.Lamone

R. Reno

A R M Y

Ravenna

R.Montone

Faenza

E I G H T H

Forli

R. Ronco

R.Savio

Cesena

R. Arno

Bibbiena

Arezzo

X Corps

E I G H T H

Rimini

Coriano

San Marino

L I N E

R. Metauro

V Corps

A R M Y

Pesaro

Ancona 15m.

Polish III Corps

Can I Corps

A D R I A T I C   S E A

British XIII Corps, now operating west of the Tiber, came up through Viterbo, and South African 6 Armoured Division, with American support, was heavily engaged east of Lake Bolsena in the battle for Bagnoregio. To the right, the advance of 78 Division persuaded the enemy to abandon Orvieto also; but thereafter, assisted by rain, German resistance stiffened. On 20 June, the pursuit came to a temporary halt, with X Corps some way north of Perugia and XIII Corps nearing the southern end of Lake Trasimene.

Fifth Army was not confronted by such difficult country, and, in the coastal sector, United States VI Corps had captured Tarquinia on 8 June and Tuscania the next day. United States IV Corps now took over from VI Corps. Farther inland, United States II Corps, on finding that the Germans had evacuated Viterbo, handed over to the French, who speedily attacked on both sides of Lake Bolsena, and on 14 June captured the town itself. The corps had now pushed on north-westward and was well beyond Arcidosso by 20 June. In the coastal sector, 36 Division of United States IV Corps had pressed on to Grosseto—evacuated by the enemy only after the mounting of a full-scale attack. While the American advance continued—Cecina being reached on 2 July—the French Corps had again moved over to the attack and on 3 July entered Siena, and continued toward Poggibonsi—where a stiff action awaited it.

In Eighth Army Sector XIII Corps was confronted by a strong defensive line based on Lake Trasimene. It was broken only after eight days of hard fighting. The corps continued its advance on the next important objective—Arezzo; but, after reaching Cortona and Castiglion Fiorentino it was halted by another strong hill position, and the check had to be accepted. North of Perugia, X Corps could achieve little in a mountainous country suitable only for infantry—until the enemy withdrawal at Trasimene spread to X Corps front. By mid-July the corps had fought its way to a commanding position east of Arezzo—entered on 16 July by XIII Corps, reinforced by New Zealand 2 Division.

Enemy opposition was still very obstinate in the difficult country west of the Arno loop, and the battle for Florence lasted for more than ten days. It was not until 4 August that South African 6 Armoured Division entered the southern outskirts of the city and reached the Arno. By 8 August, XIII Corps stood on the south bank of the river from Pontassieve, through Florence, to the right flank of Fifth Army. Meanwhile, after the fall of Arezzo, X Corps had continued its advance toward Bibbiena; and XIII Corps relieved the French Corps which, after capturing Poggibonsi, had reached a position beyond Castelfiorentino, less than ten miles from the Arno. To the west of the French, United States IV Corps had already reached Leghorn on 19 July and the mouth of the Arno on the 23rd, and occupied that part of Pisa lying south of the river.

Eighth Army's advance on the Adriatic front—which had been quiet through the winter—began as the enemy withdrew after the fall of Rome. Thus V Corps quickly reached the line of the Pescara river, and patrols were as far forward as Teramo when Polish II Corps took over, with orders to press on to Ancona. No easy passage lay ahead of the Poles, and it was 18 July—that is, after a month's fighting—before they entered the town. On 10 August they crossed the Cesano, and, ten miles on, the Metauro. By the 22nd, the corps was within assaulting distance of Pesaro, eastern end of the Gothic Line-most formidable of all the defensive 'Lines' built by the Germans in Italy. Its western end was based on Spezia.

THE GOTHIC LINE
25 August 1944–6 January 1945

Eighth Army, on the Adriatic front, struck the first blow to break the Gothic Line in order to gain entry into the plain of Lombardy. The bulk of the army was concentrated in the east for the attack, while a much depleted X Corps held a line in the mountains. The offensive opened on 25 August. Leaving the Poles to watch Pesaro, Canadian I Corps extended its front before undertaking an advance on Rimini that entailed the passage of a succession of rivers and canals. Canadian 1 Division was over the Metauro on the second day, and Canadian 5 Armoured Division joined in the pursuit to the Foglia. Here was the main belt of the Gothic Line. Nevertheless, after heavy fighting, the Canadians were over the Conca river and near Coriano by 5 September, when heavy rains checked the advance.

On the left of the Canadians, British V Corps, attacking with 46 and Indian 4 Division, made a simultaneous crossing of the Metauro; and on 29 August it joined in the battle for the Gothic Line along the Foglia. By the end of the month, like the Canadians, V Corps, with 56 Division also in the line, was over the Conca. The Marano was the next river to cross. Again because of the weather—and still stubborn enemy resistance—the corps was not to reach it until 14 September. British I Armoured Division had now reinforced the corps; and the Canadians were using the Greek Mountain Brigade alongside Canadian I Division on the coast. On the 21 St, the Canadians captured the stronghold of San Fornato; that night the Germans evacuated Rimini. Meantime British V Corps had maintained its own advance, and was now almost level with the Canadians—Indian 4 Division having cleared the enemy from the charmingly anachronistic republic of San Marino en *route*.

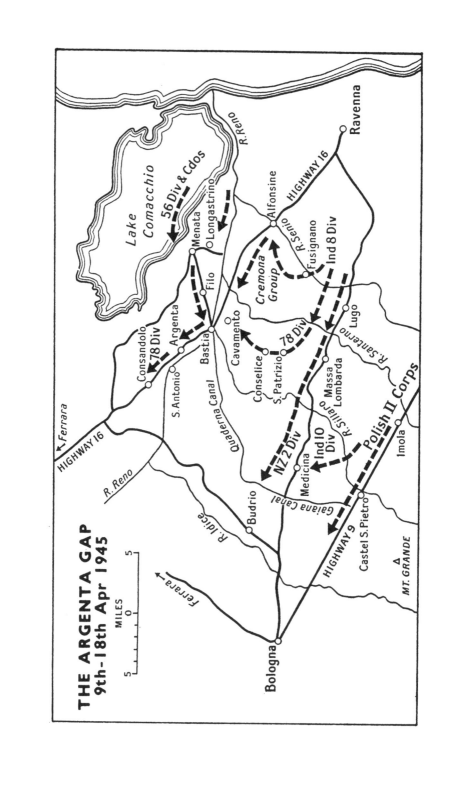

THE ARGENTA GAP
9th–18th Apr 1945

MILES

Lake Comacchio

56 Div & Cdos

R. Reno

Ravenna

HIGHWAY 16

Alfonsine

Menata

Longastrino

R. Serio

Fusignano

Ind 8 Div

Filo

Cremona Group

Lugo

Argenta

78 Div

Cavamento

78 Div

R. Santerno

Consandolo

Bastia

Conselice

S. Patrizio

Massa Lombarda

Polish II Corps

S. Antonio

Quaderna Canal

R. Sillaro

Ferrara

HIGHWAY 16

NZ 2 Div

Ind 10 Div

Imola

R. Reno

Budrio

Medicina

R. Idice

Gaiana Canal

HIGHWAY 9

Castel S. Pietro

Ferrara

MT. GRANDE

Bologna

During Eighth Army's operations the Germans had been compelled heavily to reinforce their Adriatic front, and when Fifth
Army's own advance began at the end of August they were able to
fight only rearguard actions as they withdrew. Thus it was not until
September that Fifth Army was faced by the main defences of the
Gothic Line. Its attack was launched by United States II Corps east
of the main Florence–Bologna road (Highway 65), with British XIII
Corps—under Fifth Army command—on the right flank. After a
week of hard fighting the Americans opened a route to Faenza, thus
outflanking the formidable defences of the Futa Pass. The Pass itself
was cleared on 21 September. Meanwhile the left division of II
Corps—the 34th—after attacking west of Highway 65, had
penetrated the inner defences of the Gothic Line.

British XIII Corps, now directed toward Faenza-Forli, had also
penetrated these defences in its own sector. United States IV Corps,
with South African 6 Armoured Division under command,
protected the left flank of II Corps, and followed up the Germans
retreating along the Tyrrhenian coast into the Line. While still press-
ing forward on Highway 65, the Americans launched an attack
towards Imola, along the valley of the Santerno. The advance—by
United States 88 Division—was brought to a halt among the
mountains as it approached the Imola–Bologna road at the end of
September. The Corps was now well forward of British XIII Corps,
and contact between the two corps was difficult to maintain.

The attack of United States II Corps (34, 85, and 91 Divisions)
astride Highway 65 made headway despite the mountainous country
and an obstinate defence; and after a short pause at the end of
September the offensive was resumed on a frontage of sixteen miles.
By mid-October, when sheer exhaustion compelled a relaxation of
effort, the forward troops were not more than ten miles from
Bologna. Farther west, South African 6 Armoured Division had
continued a fighting advance to cover the flank of II Corps; and
British XIII Corps, taking over the right of United States 88 Division, had made some progress in the valley of the Senio; but the
exhaustion of the troops, and the lack of reinforcement, prevented
any further effort on the part of Fifth Army—now facing winter in
the inhospitable mountains.

On Eighth Army front, after the capture of Rimini, British
V Corps continued its advance, with 1 Armoured and 46 Divisions
in the lead; but before the end of September heavy rain ruled out
for some days the possibility of movement in the coastal areas and
along the rivers. When operations were resumed, General Sir
Richard McCreery had taken over command of Eighth Army. By
20 October, having attacked left across the Apennine foothills, and

turning in succession each river line, V Corps was in Cesena after an advance by British 46 and Indian 10 Divisions; and the Canadian Corps (Canadian 1 and New Zealand 2 Divisions) had been able to reach the line of the Savio on the coastal side. Wide on the left flank, Polish II Corps continued to make progress against scattered but stiffening opposition. On 9 November, 46 Division entered Forli. By 26 November, V Corps was on the line of the Lamone river.

On 2 December, Canadian I Corps captured Ravenna and crossed the Lamone; V Corps and Polish II Corps also made the passage of the river, in face of desperate counter-attacks; on the night of the 10th the Canadians also cleared the far bank of the Lamone north and south of Bagnacavallo—but their thirst for the Senio river was checked on the line of a stoutly defended canal. Nevertheless, New Zealand 2 and Indian 10 Divisions had secured bridgeheads on the Senio by the 16th, maintaining touch with the Poles on their left; and on this same day Faenza was cleared by Indian troops. Three days later the Canadians, too, had succeeded in thrusting to the Senio and clearing its southern bank left and right.

There followed the inevitable lull for mopping-up operations— and recuperation. The Senio, in fact, was not to be crossed until 9 April 1945; and, apart from a successful attack by Canadian 5 Armoured Division in January to establish itself on the near bank of the Reno river at the south-eastern corner of Lake Commacchio, and the linking up of Canadian I Corps with British 56 Division now north of Faenza, winter—as on Fifth Army—took over on Eighth Army front. When Fifteenth Army Group again went over to the offensive, General Mark Clark had taken over command—I myself, On 12 December 1944, having moved on to the command of the Mediterranean Theatre, in succession to General Wilson.

THE ARGENTA GAP
9–18 April 1945

Eighth Army—weakened by the departure of Canadian I Corps for north-west Europe—opened the 1945 spring offensive. The advance from the line of the Senio was north-westward along Highway 16, through Argenta, where the road was one of the few dry 'gaps' in far-spread inundations, and heavily mined. Ferrara, in the plain of the Po, was the ultimate objective; but it was the intention that the left flank of Eighth Army, advancing up Highway 9, should help Fifth Army to secure Bologna. Before the launching of the main attack, two commandos on 1 April, advancing by land and by water, successfully attacked the Commachio spit, and, by 6 April, 56 Division had made progress between the lake and the Reno river.

The main attack was launched on 9 April, when New Zealand 2 and Indian 8 Divisions crossed the Senio and began an advance in concert with the Poles on the left flank. Lugo was taken, and bridgeheads were secured over the River Santerno. At Fusignano, the Italian Cremona Group—the first of several new formations raised by the Italian Government and equipped by Britain—turned east to attack Alfonsine. After occupying it, the Group rapidly advanced along Highway 16 to reach the Santerno—with the satisfaction of having helped to breach on its line of march a strong defensive position between the two rivers named by the Germans—with what intent history does not relate—the Genghiz Khan Line.

Meanwhile, on the seaward flank, a commando secured a bridgehead on the Reno at Menata. 56 Division pushed forward to Longastrino and also approached Filo on the road to Bastia. On 12 April, 78 Division passed through Indian 8 Division and turned northward: this advance, though stoutly contested, reached S. Patrizio and Conselice; on the right, Cavamento was secured. New Zealand 2 Division had now passed through Massa Lombarda, and by 14 April, was on both banks of the Sillaro river. 78 Division was on Highway 16, to become the left division of the direct assault on the Argenta Gap. 56 Division on the right had closed in and captured Filo; by the 16th it was in Bastia, and in touch with the 78th, which now took the lead in the advance along Highway 16, with the 56th coming in from the right. The battle for Argenta lasted through two days—and strong opposition to the advance of 6 Armoured and 78 Divisions was still to come at S. Antonio and Consandolo.

Away to the left, the New Zealanders had reached the Sillaro. The Poles, who had taken Imola on Highway 9, were also at the river. On the 17th, the New Zealanders reached the Gaiana Canal—beyond the Sillaro. Indian 10 Division had now come up and entered Medicina; and the Poles, after capturing Castel S. Pietro, also closed up to the Gaiana Canal—some thirteen miles from Bologna.

FINAL VICTORY IN ITALY

Fifth Army successfully opened its last offensive with a preliminary attack on 5 April up the Serchio Valley near the Ligurian coast—Carrara being evacuated by the Germans on the 11th. The main attack went in three days later, United States IV Corps striking at the enemy's mountain positions west of Highway 64 and advancing up the road itself well beyond Vergato. This success of United States IV Corps assisted United States II Corps—with South African 6 Armoured Division under command—in its fighting advance astride Highway 65. In the early morning of 20 April,

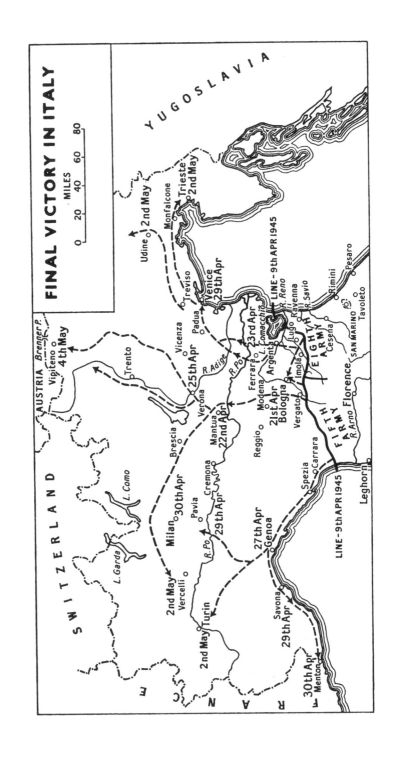

FINAL VICTORY IN ITALY

MILES
0   20   40   60   80

II Corps began to emerge from the mountains into the plain of the Po; the next day it entered Bologna.

Eighth Army had resumed its own advance on the night of 18 April, XIII Corps and Polish II Corps storming the Gaiana Canal and pushing on to the Idice river unopposed; thus the Poles were able to reach Bologna two hours ahead of the Americans. The New Zealanders continued north-westward and made contact with South African 6 Armoured Division of Fifth Army fifteen miles north-west of Ferrara. Fifth Army now held the south bank of the river for a distance of sixty miles. British V Corps—6 Armoured, 56, 78, and Indian 8 Divisions—with the enemy still strong on the ground on this front of many waterways—advanced on Ferrara, reaching it on 25 April. Eighth Army, too, was thus lined up on the Po, on a front of twenty-five miles. The actual crossing of the river presented no difficulty to the Allied armies. Two days later 6 Armoured and New Zealand 2 Divisions reached the Adige alongside Indian 8 Division, which had moved up Highway 16; near the mouth of the river the Cremona Group, assisted by partisans, cleared the countryside.

United States II Corps, after crossing the river on 25 April, moved swiftly to occupy Verona and Vicenza. At Padua—entered by British V Corps on the 29th—South African 6 Armoured Division, from Fifth Army, made contact with the Eighth. British 6 Armoured Division had also made contact with the Americans, at Treviso, and had despatched light forces on to Udine, some forty miles northwest of Trieste—where, on 2 May, the New Zealanders arrived, by way of Venice, to accept a German surrender, after encountering Yugoslav forces at Monfalcone. Away to the west, United States 92 Division, on 30 April, after reaching Genoa three days earlier, had gained contact with French troops near Menton.

Meanwhile United States 1 Armoured Division had fanned out to the shores of Lakes Garda and Como—reached on 28 April—and to Milan, entered on the 30th; and United States 10 Mountain Division had moved northward through Verona to close all routes leading to the Brenner Pass. On the morning of 4 May, two days after the formal German surrender, a column from United States Seventh Army, still at war in north-west Europe, moving south from the neighbourhood of Salzburg, joined up with a column from United States Fifth Army at Vipiteno, on the Italian side of the Brenner Pass—thus completing the tapestry of the Allied campaign in Italy.

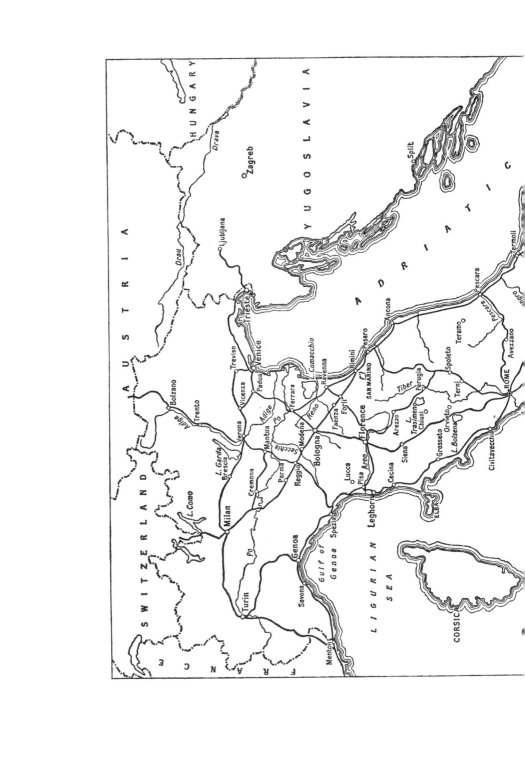

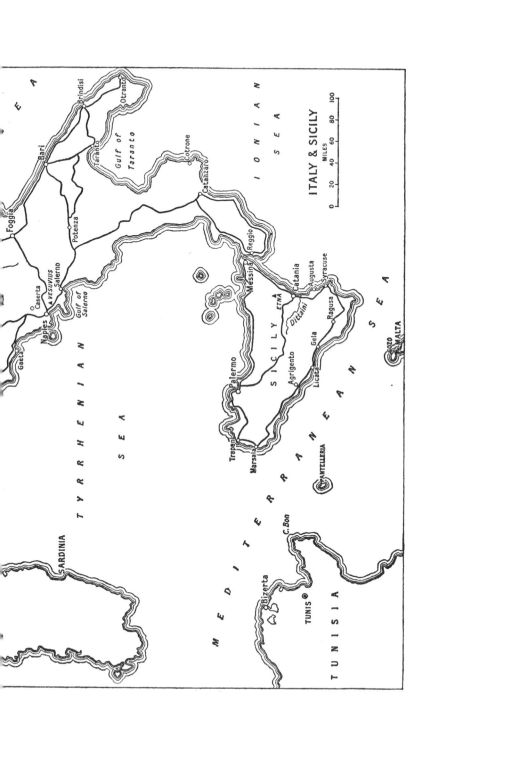

ITALY & SICILY

MILES

0 20 40 60 80 100

Index

(References in this index to the narrative of the Battle Maps are in *italic figures*)

INDEX

INDEX

to, on Eighth Army victories, 33–5; in
argument with Eisenhower, 41–2,
139; his message to Eighth Army at
Alamein, 49; his political
representative in Italy, 109–10; warns
Italy of result of helping Germans,
110; and timing of capture of Rome,
128; impatient messages of, 130; at
Yalta, 133–4; visits Italian battlefield,
137; and Greek situation, 141, 143;
offers Governorship of Canada to
Alexander, 159; after 1945 election,
160; mentioned, 119, 147, 154
Cisterna, *179*, *185*
Civita Castellana, *189*
Civitavecchia, *189*
Clark, General Mark, 42; in Italy, 45,
113, 115, 118, 126; changes direction
of break-out from Anzio, 127, *185*;
takes Rome, 127–8; in command of
Fifteenth Army Group, 154, *196*;
mentioned, 109
Clarke, Major Sir Rupert, Bt., 131
Clogher Valley Railway, 80
Commacchio, Lake, *196*
Como, Lake, 160, *199*
Conca, River, *193*
Consandolo, *197*
Conselice, *197*
Coriano, *193*
Cortona, *192*
Cossack divisions in Italy, 129
Cremona Group, *197*, *199*
Cunningham, Admiral Sir Andrew, *106*
Cyrenaica, 6–7, *58*; cleared of enemy,
32–5
Czech formations in Italy, 129

DAMASKINOS, Archbishop, 142–4
Darlan, Admiral, 34
Deir el Munassib, *51*
Delemara, 107
Delta, defence of the, 18–19
Desert Air Force, at Alam Halfa, *51*; at
Alamein, *53*; in pursuit of Afrika
Korps, *58*, *61*, *67*; in Italy, *175*
'Dragoon', Operation, 41, 43, 138–9
Dulles, Allen, 149
Dunkirk, 73–9, *86–90*, 149
Dyle, River, *86*

EBOLI, Mount, *169*
Eden, Rt. Hon. Anthony, 78–9

Eisenhower, General Dwight D., 40–4;
on Montgomery, 16; in Torch, 34;
Supreme Allied Commander, 40, *177*;
responsible for halting armies in
Italy, 41–3, 138–9; disregards political
significance of Berlin, 43–4; directive
given to (1943), 108; report to, from
Italy, 117; new directive of, 118; on
disadvantage of mixed Corps, 127–8
ELAS–EAM, 141–4
Enfidaville, 7, 33, 37, *69–71*
Engineer Combat Regiment, U.S., *185*
Enna, *165*
Escaut, River, 87
Esperia, *184*
Etna, Mount, *164*, *168*
European Advisory Commission, 43–4

FAENZA, *195–6*
Ferrara, 147–8, *196*, *199*
ffrench, O'Brien, 130
Filo, *197*
Florence, 135, *192*; hiding-place of
pictures from, 110–11
Foggia, *171*
Foglia, River, *193*
Foligno, *189*
Fondi, *184*
Fondouk Pass, 37; area, *69*
Forli, *196*
Formia, *184*
Fossacesia, *175*
Foum Tatahouine, *61*
France, German invasion of, *84–90*;
strategically useless attack on South,
136, 139–40, 146
Frascati, 129
Freyberg, Lt.-General Sir Bernard, 152,
154
Frosinone, 124, *184*, *189*
Fuka, *58*
Fusignano, *197*
Futa Pass) 136, *195*

GABES, 67, 69
Gafsa, 65, 69
Gaiana Canal, *197*, *199*
Garda, Lake, *199*
Gariliano, River, 117, 119, *173*, *177*, *184*
Gathorne-Hardy, General Sir Francis,
81
Gaulle, General Charles de, 139
Gebel Ahmera ('Longstop'), 36

INDEX

PACHINO peninsula, *165*
Padua, *199*
Palermo, 105, 107, *168*
Paliano, *189*
Panaccioni, *186*
Pantellaria, *164*
Pantha, *102*
Patton, General George S., jnr., 44–6;
  in N. Africa, 40–1, 44; in Sicily, 45,
  105, 107–8, *164, 168*
Pegu, 91–2
Persano, *171*
Perugia, *189, 192*
Pesaro, 136, *193*
Pescara, River, *193*
Pico, *184*
Piedimonte, *184*
Pignataro, *184*
Pin Chaung, *101*
Piraeus, 141–2
Pisa, *193*
Pius XII, Pope, 122
Pizzo, *169*
Plastiras, General, 144
Po River and Valley, water-lines of,
  136–7; possible objectives after con-
  quest of, 138; crossing of, 147–8, *199*
Poggibonsi, 135, *192*
Pontecorvo, 123, *184*
Potenza, *171*
Potsdam Conference, 159
Primosole bridge, *165*
Prome, *100–1*
Pyinmana, *100–1*

QATTARA Depression, 21, *49*

RAGUSA, *165*
Randazzo, *168*
Rangers, United States, 115, *169*
Rangoon, 91–3, *100*
Rapido, River, 119, *179–81*
Ravenna, 137, *196*
Reggio, *168*
Reno, River, *196*
Rimini, 136, *193*
Robertson, General Sir Brian, 158
Roccasecca, *184*
Rodzianko, Colonel Paul, 157
Romagna water-lines, 136
Rome, advance on, 116, 127–8, *186–7*;
  German resolve to hold, 117–18;
  Allied objective, 118, *171, 177*; in

Allied occupation, 122; capture of,
  128–9, *189*; German retreat from, 135
Rommel, Field-Marshal Erwin, legend
  of, 13, 15; at Alam Halfa, 24–5, *49, 51*;
  deceived by fake map, 25; defeated at
  Alamein, 26; retreat of, 29;
  reinforcements to, *60, 65*
Royal Air Force, at Salerno, 115; *see also*
  Desert Air Force
Royal Navy, evacuates Army from
  Dunkirk, 78; supports and assists
  Italian campaign, 113–14, 126–7
Rundstedt, Field-Marshal von, 76
Russia, effect of British intervention in
  Greece on German attack on, 144–5
Russian: formations with Germans in
  Italy, 129; Ambassador in Italy, 131–
  2; losses in war, 134
Ruweisat Ridge, 4, *51, 53, 56*

SAGAING, *102*
S. Antonio, *197*
S. Patrizio, *197*
Salerno, landings at, 113–15, 126, *169*;
  fighting from the beachhead, *16–173*
San Benedetto, 148
San Fornato, *193*
San Marino, *193*
San Vito, *175*
Sangro, River, 117; battle of the, 118,
  174–5
Sant' Angelo, *184*
Santerno, River, *195, 197*
Scobie, Lt.-General Ronald, 141–2
Sele, River, 115, *169–71*
Senio, River, *195*
Serchio Valley, *197*
Sfax, *69*
Shan States, *101*
Shwedaung, *101*
Shwegyin, *102*
Sicily, conquest *of*, 29, 46, 108, 158,
  162–5, 168; invasion of, 44–5, 105–7,
  164–5; Patton incident in, 45; Italian
  surrender taken in, 111
Siena, *192*
Sillaro, River, *197*
Simeto, River, *165*
Simmonds, Lt.-General Guy, 108
Sittang, *102*
Sittang River, 91, *100*
Sitwell, Sir Osbert, Bt., 110
Slim, General Sir William, 95, *100*

INDEX

Slovak formations in Italy, 129
Smuts, Field-Marshal Jan, 129
Sollum, 6, 29
Sousse, *69*
Southern Command, Alexander takes over, 15, 79–81
Spezia, 135, *193*
Stalin, Josef, 133–4
Stilwell, General Joseph ('Vinegar Joe'), 94–5, *100–1*
'Supercharge', Operation, 27–8
Syracuse, 105–7, *165*

TAKROUNA, *71*
Tamu, *102*
Taormina, *168*
Taranto, *171*
Tarhuna, *61*
Tarquinia, *192*
Taungdwingyi, *101–2*
Tebessa, *65*
Tedder, Air Chief Marshal Sir A., 106
Tennant, Admiral W. G., 79
Teramo, *193*
Termoli, *171*
Terni, *189*
Terracina, *184, 185*
Testament of Adolf Hitler, The, 77
Tharrawaddy, 93
Thoma, General von, 25
Tiber, River, *185, 189, 192*
Tito, Marshal, 132, 138–9, 152
Tobruk, *51, 59,* 60
Todt labour organization, 135
Tolbukhin, Marshal, 132–3
Tollo, *175*
'Torch', Operation, 28–9, 34, *58*
Toungoo, 91, *100*
Trapani, *168*
Trasimene, Lake, 135, *192*
Treviso, *199*
'Trident' Conference, 108, 116
Trieste, 131, 138, 151–2, *199*
Trigno, River, *171, 173, 175*
Tripoli, 32–3, 44, *58,* 60–*1*
Tripolitania, 6–7, 32–5
Troina, *168*
Truman, President Harry S., 43

Tunis, capture of, 29–30, 37–8, *71;* drive on, 32–9, *69*
Tunisia, visited in 1960, 6–7; timetable for conquest of, 29–30; campaign in, 34, 36–9, *61–70*
Tuscania, *192*

Valiant, H.M.S., *114*
Vallo, 116
Valmontone, 127, *187*
Venafro, *173*
Venice, 154, *199*
Vergato, *197*
Verona, *199*
Vesuvius, Mount, 116, *169*
Vicenza, 199
Vienna, lost opportunity of taking, 138–9
Vietinghoff, General von, 149–51
Vietri, 115–16, *169–71*
Villa Grande, *175*
Vinchiaturo, *171*
Vipiteno, 149, *199*
Viterbo, *192*
Vizzini, *165*
Volturno, River, 116, *173;* coastal plain of, 114

WADI Akarit, *67–9*
Wadi Zigzaou, *65, 67*
Warspite, H.M.S., *114*
Wavre, *86–7*
Western Desert, in 1960, 3–7; British defeat in, 12–13; H.Q. in, 14–15; fighting in, *49;* Intelligence in, 157
Wilson, General Sir Henry Maitland, 141, *177, 196*
Wingate, Maj.-General Orde, 91
'Winter Line', 117–19, *172–3, 175, 177*
Winterton, Maj.-General John, 95
Wolff, General Karl, 149

YALTA Conference, 132–4
Yenangyaung Oilfields, *101*
Yugoslavia, 132, 144, 151–2; Resistance forces of, 138–9, *199*

ZUARA, *63*